Linked Inbound

8 Social Selling Strategies to Generate Leads on LinkedIn®

by Sam Rathling

samrathling.com

LinkedInbound.co.uk

Table of Contents

Foreword by Marcus Cauchi

If you want to sell more, more often, to more people at lower cost of sale and with less effort, read and IMPLEMENT what you learn in this book.

Sam Rathling is a highly skilled LinkedIn® practitioner who has spent countless hours obsessing about every aspect of prospecting and developing your personal brand on LinkedIn®. She walks the talk as evidenced by how she used LinkedIn® to rebuild her business from scratch after she was subject to a hostile takeover in 2018. She spent a couple of months licking her wounds recovering from the emotional shock and then phoenixed her business. From a standing start, in just 6 months she has generated over $500,000 from new enterprise clients, delivering consultancy, training and coaching, applying what she knows to build her sales pipeline. We worked on a few deals together, planning, rehearsing and executing her sales plan, and she predictably closed several major deals AS A START UP.

I got to know Sam after she responded to a rant of mine because I was frustrated at not being able to do something on LinkedIn® Sales Navigator, the premium version of LinkedIn®. I, like many of you, thought I could up my game by upgrading to Sales Navigator. It wasn't as simple as that. Sam dropped me a private

4

message and offered to help me out. She fixed the problem and I was off.

I have been a LinkedIn® member since 2007 and I was doing OK on there before meeting Sam in summer 2018. I had about 4000 connections. I produce a lot of relevant content for my target audience. I don't believe you can share enough good content.

Since meeting Sam I have had a 355% increase in my levels of connections. I routinely receive inbound leads every day. I can attribute over £200,000 in new business and I landed … wait for it … a £50,000 speaking gig for 90 minutes on stage. My followers have grown by over 300% to more than 18,000. At the time of writing this foreword I rank 342% higher than the average sales trainer on LinkedIn® in my SSI (Social Selling Index) and 61% higher than the average of people in my network. My content gets much higher exposure and is shared more widely since every time a contact likes, comments or shares it, it gets shared to a proportion of their network too.

What Sam recommends in this short, practical book, works in the real world. It's not 'airy-fairy' theory. This is street fighter LinkedIn® advice. It is built on a decade and half of scar tissue. She has learned through trial and error what works and what doesn't, so you don't have to go through either the trial or the error. Pay attention to what she teaches. Get on to her 3-day Masterclass. Send your people. I recommend her to my clients and the Masterclass accelerates their learning.

Sam is an engaging trainer and I am really picky when it comes to trainers. I've suffered a lot of bad ones and been privileged to experience some of the best. Sam is up there among them. She is funny, flexible, direct and effective. Her content is great. She delivers it with structure and clarity, and it is backed up by over 25,000 hours practical, hands on experience on the platform.

She is the only LinkedIn® trainer who has the expertise to work with enterprise clients whom I can recommend confidently, because she always delivers at or above expectation.

Something else about Sam is that she has the intellectual humility to keep learning. She knows that she doesn't know it all. She is always asking the question, "How can I improve?" You want that in a trainer. "If you're green you grow, if you're ripe, you rot". LinkedIn® is constantly evolving and changing its algorithm. The market is constantly changing. And sales is changing. Sales has changed more in the past 5 years than it has in the past 50.

If you have a sales team and they are not using social selling, they are COSTING YOU MONEY. If you and your executive team are not using LinkedIn® to build your brand, attract top talent, partners, franchisees, suppliers, YOU ARE COSTING YOUR BUSINESS MONEY. Sam helps enterprise executives tackle and systemise all these problems. Read her book. Apply what you learn. Contact her and invite her into your organisation to help.

Here's quick litmus test. Take a look at your own LinkedIn®
profile and the profiles of a few of your salespeople. Do they
have a photo? That blue banner at the top of their profile page -
is it blue or does it have some form of powerful position image
that helps you stand apart? Do those profiles read like a bad CV
or do they talk about your customers and how you've helped
them? Is there any rich media on those profiles? Is the headline
bland, lazy or vanilla? If you were a potential customer, would
any of them cause you to spontaneously want to connect? Now,
have the team run their SSI score (see Chapter 1). You too. Any
sales team members with SSI scores less than 70 are definitely
losing you money.

OK, how did you fare?

If like so many executives, you are being asked to do more with
less and you're frustrated by your salespeople staring at the
phone aggressively praying it will ring, or you've outsourced your
lead generation activities to the likes of telemarketing, SEO,
email marketing, SMS marketing, advertising, or you're blaming
your marketing department for the poor lead flow, then, for a
fraction of the cost, you can use LinkedIn® for much higher
returns if you do what you will learn in this book.

You will read about how Sam has helped clients generate
$millions of qualified opportunities in the pages that follow. What
she teaches is scalable, repeatable and exceptionally cost
effective with ROI's in the tens of thousands %.

Drop her a connection request at

https://www.LinkedIn.com/in/samrathling-LinkedInexpert/

Alternatively, InMail or direct message her and arrange to speak about how she can help you and your team:

- Access and engage with key decision makers in your prime target accounts
- Build your sales pipeline
- Take business away from incumbent competitors
- Protect your own key accounts from competitive predation
- Close more new business
- Win higher value clients
- Expand sales within your existing accounts
- Make your salespeople more productive & profitable
- Fill events
- Attract top talent
- Attract the right kind of partners
- Attract better suppliers
- Expand into new markets
- Build and sustain credibility and market share
- Raise your personal brand
- Differentiate yourself and your business in a crowded, competitive, price sensitive market

If you aren't evolving you are already extinct. LinkedIn® is a tool that can help you stay current, be relevant and build your business profitably and predictably without losing control. There is no one better at helping you do that than Sam Rathling.

Marcus Cauchi

Managing Director, Sandler

Berkshire, United Kingdom

Email: mcauchi@sandler.com

Phone: +44 (0)7515 937221

LinkedIn®: https://www.LinkedIn.com/in/maximisechannelsales/

Who Should Read this Book?

Sales Directors, CEO's, Entrepreneurs, Business Owners and Experts pick up this book because they are worried about their weak sales pipeline. Despite being really good at what they do, they just don't have enough leads and really need more clients. Many are overwhelmed by just how much there is to do running their business and cannot find the time to fit LinkedIn® into their busy schedule. Most people know they need to be on LinkedIn®, but are frustrated because they don't have the knowledge to make it work and they just can't seem to get the leads into their business that they know they should be getting.

This is an easy to understand, simple and practical guide that you can implement in your business or with your sales team. You don't have a lot of time, I get it, and you want to make sure the time you do spend is on the right things. As a business owner myself, I know and appreciate the pressure you are under and believe me, if someone had given me this book at the start of my LinkedIn® journey back in 2003, I would not have had to spend years and years trying to work it out!

Everything I am about to teach you is self-taught, I have over 25,000 hours of experience in using the LinkedIn® platform, mastering the art of social selling. With over 400 leads a month coming into my business just from LinkedIn®, we implement these strategies consistently as a team; we never have to look for business, because clients come to us.

I started on my LinkedIn® journey as a Recruitment Consultant in the Netherlands. Back then LinkedIn® was a part of my daily life; I heard about LinkedIn® at a networking event and I was instantly hooked! I was an early adopter, one of the first people in Europe to have a LinkedIn® profile. Then in 2005, when I started my own recruitment agency, I also had to use LinkedIn® for lead generation and for building my personal brand.

Fast forward to today, I have now built up more than 9 years' experience teaching LinkedIn® to thousands of people across 23 countries. I am the most sought-after LinkedIn® Expert in Europe, my diary is booked out months in advance and I deliver keynotes to packed out rooms all around the world. I run sold out Social Selling Masterclasses every month in my head office in the East Midlands in the UK. My team of LinkedIn® ninjas are set up to do the work for our clients who simply don't have the time to do it themselves.

"Linked Inbound" was written as an easy to understand, simple and practical guide that will be effective for your business and take very little time to implement. LinkedIn® is an amazing business tool. Whether you are selling B2B or B2C, you really can generate massive opportunities, new leads and clients.

11

You will really like this book and benefit hugely from it if:

- You have no profile at all on LinkedIn® and are starting from scratch
- You have a profile on LinkedIn® but can't remember the last time you looked at it!
- You are using LinkedIn® already but currently do not get any business from it
- You have limited time to spend on LinkedIn® and need to know the daily habits
- You are ready to take your online reputation and your business to the next level
- You want to position yourself as the 'go-to' expert in your field
- You know your target market is on LinkedIn® but you have no clue how to gain access to them
- You have employees to whom you could replicate this advice
- You have less than 15 minutes a day to spend on networking sites like LinkedIn®
- You have heard of 'Social Selling', but don't really know what it is or how to turn LinkedIn® into real leads and sales opportunities
- You work in an organisation that has invested in LinkedIn® Sales Navigator for your sales team

This book was written for every individual who knows the huge potential of LinkedIn®, but has no idea how to unlock it. Well... I am about to give you the key.

If you put aside 1 hour a week for the next 90 days you would be able to completely revamp your LinkedIn® presence and start to see an increase in visits to your profile, an increase in the number of people attracted to your profile and a significant increase in the amount of times you show up in search results.

LinkedIn® marketing and social selling is a marathon, not a sprint. It takes consistency and patience. This is not a magic bullet or a quick fix, but if you implement what I share with you in the book and follow the daily and weekly habits I give you in Chapter 11, you can be sure to become better at 'social selling' (more on that later). You will get real clarity on your target market, who they are and how to start real conversations with them. Over time you will generate inbound leads, grow your personal brand and prospect effectively to build your sales pipeline.

My purpose in writing this book is simple... I want to help you win more clients, and the more you implement from this book, the better your chances of securing new leads from LinkedIn®, which is why you picked this book in the first place.

If you are a Sales Director or Business Owner, I have written this with your team in mind, so if you do employ staff or a sales team, then every single one of them should also implement these tips on their own LinkedIn® profile. Why not gift this book to every employee as a thank-you for their hard work, and in return your business will massively benefit from the maximum exposure you will get!

Having an increased online presence and a wider network from each of your team will really give you an added edge over your competitors. You never know, you may find a LinkedIn® whizz in the team who fancies taking on more responsibility in this area and could really ramp up your LinkedIn® presence as a business.

Let's get started with the social selling framework that I have developed, with 8 strategies to help you win big on LinkedIn®.

8 Social Selling Strategies

At the time of writing, my Social Selling framework has generated close to £10million in closed business for my clients in 12 months. I am on a mission to generate over £1billion for my clients by 2025.

Whether someone picked up this book, just like you did, attended a 1-Day Workshop with me or invested in a 3 Day Social Selling Masterclass, this framework is responsible for changing businesses on a global level.

I am excited to share the details behind this model and help you to truly understand how to unlock the power of LinkedIn® for your sales pipeline. I will address each one of these 8 strategies in this book, starting with key principles and working my way around the wheel, clockwise.

8 Social Selling Strategies

CHAPTER 1
Principles of Social Selling

There are 3 main overriding principles to focus on when it comes to social selling through LinkedIn®.

1. The VCO process

2. Understanding your Social Selling Index

3. The Power of 'Givers Gain'

I am going to explore each of these in detail to get you thinking about how you can apply social selling in your business.

The VCO Process

It is vital that you understand the VCO Process if you are to be successful at marketing your business through LinkedIn®. This process is usually referred to when we talk about referral marketing, when networking on a face to face basis, and the key is in the power of relationships. The system of information, support and referrals that you assemble from your networks, both online and offline, will be based on your relationships with other individuals and businesses. Referral marketing works because these relationships work both ways and both parties benefit in some way.

The relationship evolves through three phases: Visibility, Credibility and Opportunity. We call this evolution the VCO Process. First you and your business must be visible. Your LinkedIn® profile is your 24/7 digital ambassador, working for you around the clock. This is all about you having a presence online, having a personal profile and a company profile and being seen to be active and engaged on LinkedIn®. Visibility comes from posting great content, having a great profile and being an active member of the LinkedIn® community.

Next, comes Credibility, it is not enough to be visible. People have got to know, like and trust you before they are going to part with their money. Always keep in mind that any successful relationship, whether a personal or a business relationship, is unique to every pair of individuals, and it evolves over time. The relationship starts out tentative, fragile, full of unfulfilled possibilities and expectations. It grows stronger with experience and familiarity, and then it matures into trust and commitment.

Credibility online, especially on LinkedIn® is all about how you and your business come across to others, how you start and build relationships, how you position yourself through your profile and in the way you approach relationship building and growing your network.

The VCO Process describes the process of creation, growth and strengthening of business, professional and personal relationships. The main problem with people's lack of understanding of this vital process is that they forget the step that involves the 'C', credibility is all about growing and nurturing the relationship before moving to a sale or moving into a place where someone will refer you to one of their clients. All too often we see people using LinkedIn® as a selling platform, spamming their network with requests to buy products or services from them, or visit their website. The credibility part is vital if you want to grow your business on LinkedIn®. Rushing into selling destroys your credibility and you may never recover.

Only when you add Visibility to Credibility can you move to Opportunity and Profitability in a relationship. When you move the relationship to the next level you will be referred, recommended, promoted and will spread great word of mouth about you and your business. When you are networking online, the VCO Process is even more important as you may not get the chance to actually meet the person you are networking with on a face to face basis.

Always bear in mind that Visibility + Credibility = Opportunity. This simple concept has made a bigger difference in more people's networking efforts than any other single idea you will come across and should be remembered as you read this book.

Almost every tip in this book is going to relate to either Visibility or Credibility, and in many cases, both will apply.

Your Social Selling Index (SSI)

What is Social Selling?

According to Wikipedia, Social Selling is the process of developing relationships as part of the sales process. It is about leveraging your social network to find the right prospects, build trusted relationships, and ultimately, achieve your sales goals.

This sales technique enables better sales lead generation and sales prospecting process and eliminates the need for cold calling. Building and maintaining relationships is easier within the network that you and your customer trust.

Prospecting, lead generation and pipeline building via traditional methods are failing. Social selling gives you a competitive edge that gets you seen by your target market.

According to LinkedIn®, social selling leaders create **45%** more opportunities than peers with a lower SSI. Social selling leaders are **51%** more likely to reach quota and **78%** of social sellers outsell peers who don't use social media.

Your Social Selling Index

Whether you know this, or not, you have a score out of 100 called a Social Selling Index. It is available for free and can help you to benchmark how you are currently performing on LinkedIn®. The higher your SSI, the higher the chance you will generate leads and real business opportunities. Open LinkedIn® on your desktop, then open a new tab and go to the link below. If checking from a mobile, then visit: http://LinkedIn.com/sales/ssi on your browser and you will find out your own SSI score.

"Social Selling is the Art of Selling without Selling"

Sam Rathling

You will see an overall score out of 100, this is your SSI as of today, a copy of mine is here for reference. This is updated every 24 hours, and once you know how to move the needle on each section you can make dramatic improvements with limited time input. It will look something like this:

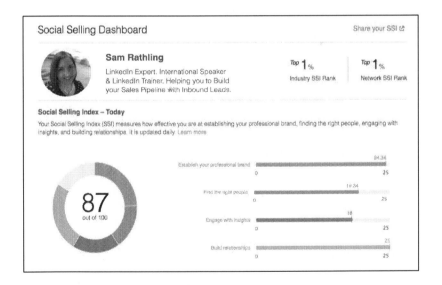

Ideally you should be aiming for 75+ as this is where the LinkedIn® magic happens! If you are already over 70 then you are doing an amazing job and there are some small tweaks to be made. If you are less than 50, don't panic, that is after all the reason you came looking for this book. Within 90 days or so of consistent action we can get you to 75+.

How is my Social Selling Index Made Up?

There are 4 areas of focus, all equally weighted 25 points. LinkedIn® uses this score to push you towards their premium, paid for services. You can still score over 70 with the free version of LinkedIn®, however to truly elevate your SSI and head into the high 80s and 90s you will need to use Sales Navigator to master the art of social selling in the LinkedIn® environment. Your SSI score is made up of 4 sections, under the following headings:

Establish your Professional Brand (Orange)

Find the Right People (Purple)

Engage with Insights (Red)

Build Relationships (Green)

Let's look at each one in more detail as they make up your overall SSI score.

SSI - Establish your Professional Brand
(Orange Section)

There are 7 main areas within this part of your SSI:

- How Complete your LinkedIn® Profile is
- Multimedia Links in your Profile About section & Work Experience
- Projects and Publications section completed
- Skills and Endorsement section filled out
- Regular Posts, Articles and Content, Creating followers of your Content
- Profile Picture and Banners
- Give Endorsements and Get Endorsements

The more complete your LinkedIn® personal profile, and the more great content you post to position yourself as a 'go-to' expert in your field, the higher your orange score will be. This in turn will help you to establish your professional brand.

SSI - Find the Right People (Purple Section)

There are 6 main areas within this part of your SSI:

- Use Sales Navigator. For me Sales Navigator is like the Formula 1 Car of LinkedIn®, the problem is that most sales professionals have no idea how to drive it! Having a Sales Navigator licence will help to raise your score

- Focus on people searches, using the advanced search feature on Sales Navigator or if you are on the premium version, use searches and filters to find people in your target market and add them to your network. This will be covered later

- Viewing profiles of other people in your target market will help your SSI score to go up, you need to be engaged with looking for the right people

- In addition to you finding other people, you will also score when you generate inbound views to your own profile. The higher the number of profiles you have of the right people, the more your score will increase. You can find this number on the dashboard within your LinkedIn® profile. It's a 90-day statistic

- Saving leads in Sales Navigator is something you can only do in Navigator. Not only can you find people, you can also save them as leads and follow their activity and posts. They won't know that you have saved them as a lead, but this is a very useful exercise to do on key prospects

- Daily activity on LinkedIn® or Sales Navigator, will help your score to go higher; being an active user and logging in daily will increase this score. Consistency is key

The more prospecting you do, adding the right people into your LinkedIn® network, the higher the score will be for the purple section of your SSI.

SSI - Engage with Insights (Red Section)

This is one of the hardest areas to make an impact on, and for many people is often their lowest scoring area. So here are some key pointers on how to increase your 'Engage with Insights' score:

- Engagements given and received: LinkedIn® is looking at how much engagement you are receiving and giving on posts and articles

- Create content and feed the newsfeed with great posts

- Share the content of others on your newsfeed

- Publish articles and engage with people who like, comment and share your content

- Join LinkedIn® Groups, be an active member in Groups to engage with insights in groups

- Regularly save Accounts (Companies) inside of Sales Navigator

- Regularly view Account Pages and scroll the homepage of Companies (Accounts) within LinkedIn® Sales Navigator

SSI - Build Relationships (Green Section)

The Green section of your LinkedIn® SSI is all about building trusted relationships and is usually the section that scores the highest for most people.

Here are some pointers to help you to raise your SSI in the area of relationships:

- Build relationships with Decision Makers

- Engage and start conversations with people who comment and like your posts

- Prospect regularly, start conversations to build the relationship with people in your target market

- Stay on top of your LinkedIn® inbox and messages, and if you have Sales Navigator do the same on your Sales Navigator inbox

- This next one is related to Sales Navigator and InMails only - the messages you send and the % response rate you get from InMails. I am not a huge InMail fan, as it comes across as a sales pitch when you use this feature, but can help to move this score

It is usually the easiest part of your SSI to score the highest on. Use this space to write in your SSI score as of today:

My current SSI score is: _____

My target SSI is: _____

Social Selling History

The University of British Columbia first established the science of social selling during research. They found that where there are incidental similarities between a buyer and seller, it is more likely a purchase would take place.

For example, if two people follow the same sports team, they are more likely to feel a connection. The use of social technology can be used to discover incidental similarities and thus create a quicker bond with the potential client.

Whilst the University of British Columbia discovered the science, it was Nigel Edelshain who was first to put the science into practice and coined the term sales 2.0. Social selling has become increasingly popular since companies have looked to increase their return on investment in or by social media interaction.

Social Selling visionary, Koka Sexton was interviewed and spoke about how salespeople can use social media to leverage their connections to gather insights and build relationships. Sexton stated that the art of social selling is said to speed up many sales processes, whilst also improving relationships.

Social Selling in Enterprise

Sales teams within organisations frequently mine data from social media that may help them connect to customers, in order to create a more genuine sales lead. The technique frequently focusses on approaching potential clients in a less direct way, so their daily lives are not interrupted by cold calls and the hard sell 'selling without selling'.

Through my work with corporate clients, it is evident that multinational companies are becoming increasingly involved in implementing social selling at the enterprise level. According to IBM, a company that integrates social media into their business model is one that embraces and cultivates a spirit of collaboration and community throughout its organisation—both internally and externally. IBM piloted a social selling program in

2012 that is widely regarded as one of the most successful early examples of effective social selling at the enterprise level.

According to the *Social Selling Maturity Model*, a prevalent theory on social selling, there are a variety of ways enterprises engage social media or selling. These stages include allowing employees to use social media at will, enacting general policies, training employees on effective use, and deploying software designed to improve the social selling process. Enabling social selling within enterprise is a journey and very few enterprises have succeeded.

The success of socially centred selling depends on adoption of systems, for which an organisation needs to follow a structured approach. I am privileged to work with a range of multi-billion $$ enterprise clients who are embracing social selling in their overall sales strategy.

So now you know the importance of Social Selling, let's get stuck into the main content of the book so you can start the tactical implementation of each element of my 8 Social Selling Strategies.

The Power of "Givers Gain"

Networking, whether you do so online or offline, is all about finding out how you can help people and then doing it! Always focus on how you can help another connection first, remember that you first need to build credibility by relationship building;

helping the other person in some way could be connecting them to someone in your network or sharing an article that will help them and is relevant to their business.

This is widely known as "Givers Gain"® which is the philosophy of Business Network International or BNI as it is widely known as. BNI is the largest and most successful referral organisation in the world with over 259,000 members worldwide in over 70 countries. Givers Gain is based on Emerson's Law of Compensation - to get more, give more.

I am very passionate about BNI, and have helped members across the UK and in 16 other countries to grow their business through the power of giving. One of my favourite quotes is from the late Zig Ziglar. "If you help enough other people to get what they want, you will get what you want in return."

Taking this concept to LinkedIn®, if you help enough other people in your network it will all come back to you; this is based on the old adage of 'what goes around, comes around'. If you love online networking using sites like LinkedIn®, then you will also love BNI.

We recommend that you find a local chapter of BNI and go along to see how it could help your business to grow. If you are new to networking or if you want to learn how to be a more effective networker, this could be a huge opportunity for your business.

I am so passionate about this subject, that I wrote a book on the topic. You can get your copy of 'Give: 16 Giving Strategies to Grow Your Business' on Amazon just by finding my name. It has multiple 5-star reviews and has been endorsed by the Godfather of business networking, and the Founder of BNI, Dr. Ivan Misner.

The best way I can describe the power of 'Givers Gain' to you is by sharing my best LinkedIn® 'Givers Gain' story. In February 2018, I was tagged in a post on LinkedIn® by a connection who thought I might be able to help. Marcus Cauchi, was having some challenges with the LinkedIn® Sales Navigator product. He had been on a rant on the LinkedIn® newsfeed, frustrated that he couldn't make something work in his searches.

Seeing the post and his need for help, I jumped on to the comments and sent him a direct LinkedIn® message and offered to help him solve the problem. Within a few minutes I had Marcus on a video conference, shared my screen with him and quickly solved his issue.

As soon as I had helped Marcus, he asked the most common question when you've been helping someone else. "Sam, how can I help you?". Having looked at Marcus' LinkedIn® profile, I saw that he was a Sales Trainer and with over 400 articles on his subject and a substantial LinkedIn® network, I knew that this would be a potentially mutually beneficial relationship.

I explained to Marcus that I work very well with Sales Trainers, as we help our clients create leads, but don't teach them how to close the business. So we arranged a time to speak and get to learn more about how we could help each other.

Fast forward to today, Marcus is now a client and we help him to manage all of his own LinkedIn® prospecting. He builds his sales pipeline with Channel Chiefs, Channel Managers and CEO's of scale up technology companies who are looking for serious growth.

I am now a client of Marcus and am immersed in learning sales techniques with Sandler Sales Training which has transformed the way I sell and increased my conversion rates to over 90%, whilst significantly reducing my sales cycle. I now close multi-six figure contracts with corporate clients and have transitioned successfully into the Enterprise space.

Marcus and I have built a very strong referral partnership where we both refer clients to each other, and as of writing this book I can attribute over £250,000 in sales to having met Marcus last year, through LinkedIn®.

I would like to personally thank Marcus, for writing the foreword to this new edition of 'Linked Inbound'. I am so glad that we met. I feel so privileged to work with him as my mentor and I value our friendship dearly.

Know your Target Market

Before tackling any kind of social selling, especially on LinkedIn®, you need to truly understand your target market.

Most companies could service a wide range of industry sectors, types of company and given the opportunity would jump at the chance for any kind of new business. Often when I ask people to describe their target market they usually start with "anyone who…" or tell me that they are a "one stop shop…" or use "anybody that needs a XXX…" which is essentially nobody!

There are some key considerations to look at when you are focusing on your target market, these include:

Job Title – on whom do you want to focus within the companies you are targeting?

Industry – in what sectors do you have experience and can add the most value?

Geography - where ideally would you like them to be located, given the choice?

Age - how established do you want your target clients to be?

Size of Company - what size do you want the company to be in headcount of staff?

Type of Business - is it a micro-business, an SME or a multinational, privately owned?

Values - what values does your ideal client hold personally and professionally?

Ambitions - what are they looking to achieve with their company?

Take some time to think about this and write this down. The success of every strategy I am going to give you in this book hinges on you knowing, really knowing, and understanding your target market.

You may have 2 or 3 target markets. I have a range of products and services that suit a micro-business just starting out; then I have products and services that suit SMEs and I also have solutions for multinational corporate clients. I have done this exercise for each one. I have a really clear picture of what each one looks like and then I have a Top 100 list for each target market. I am VERY clear on who I want to do business with and all my social selling and marketing efforts are based on knowing my target market inside out. This then feeds my LinkedIn® profile, my content delivery and my marketing efforts across all of my social media channels.

I created a model called the IDEAL client template to help you with this. When you complete this exercise, write out a description of your ideal client. Not the clients you have at the moment, the ones you really want in the future.

Use this table to complete the IDEAL template for your own business (you may need to complete one for each target market):

Your Target Market

I - Industries Verticals, Sectors, Types of Business	
D - Demographic Size of Company, Years Established, Staff, Revenue	
E - Experience Job Titles, Background, Role and Responsibility	
A - Attributes Values, Ambitions, Culture	
L - Location Geography, Towns, Cities, Regions	

This IDEAL client framework can help you narrow your focus and think about these 5 core areas for your IDEAL client:

I   **Industries:** Verticals, Sectors, Types of Business

D   **Demographic**: Size, Years Established, Staff, Revenue

E   **Experience:** Job Title, Background, Role & Responsibility

A   **Attributes:** Values, Ambitions, Culture

L   **Location:** Geography, Towns, Cities, Regions

Your Client's PAINS

Now that you know more about what your target market looks like, it's important that you also think about the solutions that you provide for them. This starts by you truly understanding their pain points, challenges and problems.

- What problems do you solve?
- Why do clients come to you?
- What frustrations do they have?
- What challenges cause them to need your products and/or services?
- What kind of payoff do they want?
- What do they want to improve?

You hear these daily from prospects. They come up in every phone call and every meeting that you undertake with a potential client. So now take the time to write them down so that you can capture these and build them into your profile and content when I cover this later.

PAINS Profile for your IDEAL client

To help you, I have developed a PAINS profile template for you to complete, when you do so, have your IDEAL client template at the forefront of your mind.

P - Problems
What problems do you solve for your clients?

A - Agony
What keeps them awake at night?

I - Issues
What are some of the symptoms and issues?

N - Nagging
What annoys or frustrates them?

S - Struggles
What do they struggle with?

P **Problems:** What problems do you solve for your clients?

A **Agony:** What keeps them awake at night?

I **Issues:** What are some of the symptoms and issues?

N **Nagging:** What annoys or frustrates them?

S **Struggles:** What do they struggle with?

Additional Resources

The best book I can recommend to you on the topic of pain points and target market is "Making Channel Sales Work" by Marcus Cauchi and David Davies. They have a whole section on this topic, including the CAPS template within the Sandler Sales system as well as SO many more sales nuggets.

CAPS stands for:

- Characteristics
- Alternatives
- Pain Points
- Symptoms

Marcus delves deep into this topic and has helped me to really develop a clear CAPS to give me a true picture of my target market and how I help to solve their biggest frustrations. What I have learnt is that the REAL problem is never the problem that they bring you. There is always an underlying, emotion fuelled reason for them speaking with you.

When you have clear picture of your target market and a strongly developed CAPS, everything on LinkedIn® becomes SO much easier! When I deliver masterclasses and workshops this is the first thing I focus on with delegates. Why? Because it is so fundamental to social selling success.

CHAPTER 2
Powerful LinkedIn®
Profile

Your LinkedIn® profile is your digital ambassador, representing you and your business 24 hours a day, 7 days a week, 365 days a year. It is networking when you are asleep, when you are in meetings and even when you are on holiday! In many cases your LinkedIn® profile will be the very first thing that a prospect sees when they go looking for you.

A really effective LinkedIn® profile can be the difference between you winning a client or the prospect going to your competition. Think about your ideal client, I mean your absolute dream client. Now look at your LinkedIn® profile.

The most important question to ask is…

"Would you become a customer of you, based on your current LinkedIn® profile?"

If you are like most people I speak to, the answer would be no. So this chapter is dedicated to helping you to get your LinkedIn® profile right.

There are 13 areas of your LinkedIn® profile that need your attention. They are listed below:

1. Use the Right Name

Make sure that the name you use on LinkedIn® is actually the name people know you by in business, and matches the name they would search for you on LinkedIn®. That way there can be no confusion especially if you don't have a unique name. If you prefer to be called Terence by clients but everyone knows you as Terry then choose the first name that you are most likely to be searched by or the name that fits with your current online profile.

In addition make sure that your business card matches your LinkedIn® name, so if you meet someone at an event and they go to connect with you on LinkedIn® afterwards, you can be found easily. Sounds simple, however an apostrophe in the wrong place or a double-barreled name can be the difference between you making a connection and someone not bothering because they couldn't find you easily.

2. 100% Profile Complete - Become an *ALL STAR*

The initial goal of any LinkedIn® Personal profile is 100% completion, any number less than 100% is simply saying 'I couldn't be bothered'. Less than 100% affects your credibility and this also impacts upon your power to attract new connections.

Make sure that each and every section of your profile is complete, from your education to your work history, your skills,

41

summary and headline. The other reason for this is the accuracy level you will start to see when LinkedIn® begins recommending 'People You May Know'.

This 'People You May Know' feature appears in a few places on LinkedIn® and is based on the information which you enter into your Personal Profile. If you do not complete your profile then you have less chance of connecting with someone you know well, who could lead you to a new client or a great big piece of business you were not expecting.

3. Your Professional Headline

Your LinkedIn® Professional Headline, when written well, can drive massive opportunities your way, whether that be job offers or new clients. The reality is that most people use this part of their LinkedIn® profile to demonstrate their current job title or position and their company name.

The professional headline of your LinkedIn® profile is the one short description, 110 characters in length that you can see underneath your name on your profile. It is also what others see when you post an update or when you ask someone to connect with you.

Look at your current professional headline on LinkedIn®. If it says your job title or position and company name, be prepared to transform your LinkedIn® visibility. It is important if you want to get hired for a job or develop new business for your company. This one part of your profile will determine how many times you appear in search results.

It will also determine how many people will want to connect with you and is your chance to set you apart from the competition. By changing these 110 characters to include what you offer and what you want to be found for, you will change your visibility, credibility and profitability on LinkedIn®.

The Importance of Keywords and the Professional Headline

As with all web-based content, your LinkedIn® Professional Headline is keyword searchable. Pick one main keyword or phrase that you want to be found for. Have you got one? Now go to LinkedIn® and put in a people search with that keyword or key phrase in the top right corner. Did you appear on the first page? If not then the person who is in the top spot is probably getting the clients that you want!

How Should I write my Headline?

Choose your keywords wisely and you could rocket up the search rankings instantly and appear on the first page of LinkedIn® searches. We recommend that you include the keyword or keyword phrase you have picked out, at least twice in your Professional Headline. Make sure these same keywords or

43

keyword phrase also appear in other parts of your LinkedIn®
profile as well, especially in your current job title.

What else can I do to Improve my Professional Headline?

Focusing on the end benefit to the customer is another good way
to grab attention. Always remember to include the
keyword/search term twice:

Example 1:

Old Headline: *"Nutritionist"*
New Headline: *"The Nutritionist Who Increases Staff Happiness
– Nutritionist who reduces absenteeism in the workplace"*

Example 2:

Old Headline: *"Recruitment Consultant"*
New Headline: *"Changing the way the world does recruitment,
saving you time and money with fixed price, low cost recruitment"*

Example 3:

Old Headline: *"Business Coach"*
New Headline: *"Business Coach helping work less hours and
make more money! Business Coach for Entrepreneurs"*

The easiest way to think about this is to answer the question,
what does my client get AFTER they have done business with

me? What do they feel, think or say after you have delivered your product or service to them? Think about the benefits to the client and focus on that in your headline.

In summary your professional Headline should feature your main keyword twice, the earlier in the headline the better. It must read well i.e. not look like it's stuffed full of keywords and the same keyword must also feature in your summary.

5. Your Photograph

I was once asked to introduce a connection of a good business contact to one of my best clients. As I always do, I went to check the person's profile out on LinkedIn®. The first thing I saw was his photograph. It was of a scruffy looking man, in a string vest in his garden. This was a person looking to be connected with my number one multinational corporate client, and yet he chose that photograph to appear on his business profile.

It sounds obvious, I know, but your professional photograph should be exactly that... professional. In a smart business suit, regardless of your trade or profession and taken by a professional photographer, preferably with a friendly and inviting picture. You only get one chance to make an impression on LinkedIn®.

Your headshot should be head and shoulders only to comply with LinkedIn®'s guidelines, and now you can even edit your photograph and change the filters. Just click the blue pen to edit the top section of your profile, and another blue pen icon will appear next to the photograph.

6. Your Public URL

Your public URL is the small blue link that appears at the bottom of your LinkedIn® profile. This is generated by LinkedIn® and quite often contains random numbers and letters. You can edit this to make it match your name or business name.

Change the public URL to your name or your name and business name. To get to your public profile, when you are in the desktop version of LinkedIn®, click to view your profile and in the top right you will see a place to 'Edit your Public Profile'.

I have used the following public URL and have included my main keyword in mine.

https://www.LinkedIn.com/in/samrathling-LinkedInexpert/

Once you have a public URL you are happy with, you can then use this link to drive visits and connections from your email signature, your website, your business card and other social media channels. If you are just starting out in business and don't have a website yet, you can use this link to give people a place to learn more about you and your business.

Simply add a hyperlink and send them to your public profile URL. See mine below… I look forward to being connected with you and adding value to your network.

Connect with me on LinkedIn®

7. Your 'About' Section

This is the section directly underneath your photograph and contact details. You can add an 'About' section, which is a summary about you and your business and/or career; this is under-utilised by so many on LinkedIn®.

The MOST important thing to bear in mind, is that the profile should be written with your exact target market in mind. I have already covered this in the first section of this book. Imagine that your dream client is reading your profile, they click on the 'About' section and they read **2000 characters** demonstrating your credibility, how you specialise in helping people just like them, how you understand their challenges and how you can help them.

The problem with most LinkedIn® 'About' sections, is that they either read like a CV, don't have enough information or are all about the person who wrote the profile and not the target market / end client they are trying to attract. After reading this book you will notice just how many awful LinkedIn® profiles there are out there. The good news is, that most of your competitors have a poor LinkedIn® profile, so just making this one change to your 'About' section will have a noticeable impact on your profile views, search appearances, visibility and credibility.

I have provided a general structure for building your 'About' section below. Keep it to 3-4 sentences per paragraph. Make a great first impression, especially in the first 3 lines as this is the only part of your 'About' section that is shown to people when they arrive on your profile. They can choose to 'See More…' but only if the first few lines compels them to do so.

Structure of your 'About' Section

Paragraph 1 – This needs to be punchy and have impact. It needs to have your most important credibility building information, including elements like your mission or reason why you do what you do. It's your short introduction to who you are that should compel people to click on that vital 'See More…' button to open up your entire 'About' section.

Paragraph 2 – Remember that people don't care what you do! They care about the results that you get for them AFTER you do what you do. Focus this paragraph on the client's pain points, why they come to you, what problems / challenges do you solve? This is all about the pain of your customers, demonstrating to a prospective client reading your profile that you understand them and the challenges they are facing.

Paragraph 3 – Who do you Serve? Describe your target market. The more specific you can be in this paragraph the better. If you are B2B (business to business) then use descriptions including job titles, industry sectors, locations, and if you are allowed to, mention some key clients that you already work with. This is about the prospective client seeing that they fit with you and you already have experience with companies like theirs.

If you are B2C (business to consumer), then describe the demographics, life stages and events that may be occurring for them, gender if relevant, career level, family situation, locality, just be clear about who is your ideal target market, without using the words 'Anybody who…'. The key to this paragraph is the prospective client, reading your profile resonates with the description.

Paragraph 4 – What makes you different and unique? Now this is an area of your profile that you may struggle with, especially if you have never dug deep into this topic before.

This paragraph should include the things that you can say, but no competitor can say. In other words, you should not be saying things like, "we provide really good customer service". Anyone can say that! This should include awards that you have won, personally and in the business itself, unique selling points that might start with "we are the only…".

49

Paragraph 5 – Contact Details, although these appear in the contact section (covered later in this chapter), you do need to make it really obvious how to reach you. If someone reads your profile and they want to talk, then you need to make it easy for them! It might read something like this. "Message me here on LinkedIn®, call 01332 653659 or email me on hello@LinkedInbound.co.uk.

Paragraph 6 – Specialities: this is simply a list of all of your main keywords to help you get found for what you do. Don't go overboard, stick to 10-15 of your main keywords. There are many keyword tools available to help you with keywords, you probably already use many of these on your website to get you to rank on Google searches. Think about what keywords people would use to find someone like you.

8. Your Experience

The section covering your previous positions and jobs is important because it allows LinkedIn® to suggest potential connections for you based on where you have worked before. Make sure you complete this but don't write a novel under each heading, just a few lines. The one to focus on would be your current role. This is an area for you to add more keywords, explain in more detail about your products and services and expand upon what you actually do in your role. This should be different to your 'About' section.

9. Add Skills to your Profile

LinkedIn® allows you to add Skills to your profile for which you can then be endorsed. The trick with skills is to keep it to the skills for which you actually want to be endorsed; you probably have 100 different skills that you are good at to some extent. If you want to be credible and get known for being great in a particular area then restrict your skills list to the 25 or 30 core skills that you would be happy for someone to endorse you for.

Also bear in mind that skills you once had may not be relevant to what you do now, so always keep this list up to date and add or remove skills from time to time.

This list will be used by people in their searches for people with relevant skills; it is a tool most useful for recruiters and head-hunters, less relevant for business owners. However it is important that you list skills and that you can then be endorsed by others for having those skills.

10. Add Media Links to your Profile

Media links can be added to your profile to add visual impact to your LinkedIn® profile. You can add PDF's, Word documents, presentations, videos and Images to both your LinkedIn® 'About' section as well as each individual work experience section of your profile.

When you initially look at someone's LinkedIn® profile you can see the first 3 lines of their 'About' section as well as their media links, most people are visual and will gravitate towards the media. If you leave this out, you are missing a huge opportunity to give your LinkedIn® profile additional credibility. I recommend that you add at least 6-12 media links to your 'About' section, each media item that you add should support the words you have used in your LinkedIn® profile.

When you click on the blue pen in your 'About' section, you can either 'Upload' a document or 'Add a Link'. To add a video to your media section you can only use a link, so choose a YouTube link or Vimeo link. You cannot upload an original MP4 file. For all other file types, you can upload the document or image directly to your profile.

For example, if you are running events, you can add links to your booking pages to drive people to your booking pages. If you are using sales funnels or landing pages, you can add links to your profile, send them to your website or to lead capture pages, to then move people to your mailing list.

The idea here, should be that someone visiting your LinkedIn profile should be able to find out as much about you as possible from your media section, without having to leave the LinkedIn® platform. They should be given enough information on your profile through text and media for them to make a decision about a) connecting with you and b) doing business with you.

11. Add Publications & Projects to your Profile

If you have written and published books, articles, papers etc. then you can now add these to your profile. If your publication is available online, you can add links to your profile to drive sales; this is one way to give you books more exposure. In addition, publishing papers or articles raises your credibility, so the more publications you have that you can link through your profile, the better you will be positioning yourself as an expert in your field.

12. Add Voluntary Experience to your Profile

When people look at your profile, most of what they read is all about you as a business professional. After all, LinkedIn® is a business networking platform, however you can add some personal details to your profile which contain details of your philanthropic work, or voluntary work raising awareness for causes and charities that you support. If you are involved in any voluntary or community work you can share this on your LinkedIn® profile, if you have a JustGiving.com account then why not add this to your voluntary section and use LinkedIn® as an additional way to raise funds.

13. Contact Section

I know this sounds very obvious, but make sure that you contact information is correct within your LinkedIn® profile. You can edit this using the blue pen on your profile in the top right underneath your header image. Within this section there is the option to also edit your contact information.

If you want to change the email address, this is defaulted to the email you use to login to LinkedIn®, so you would need to change that in your privacy settings.

When you are adding your website to your LinkedIn® profile, the standard way to do this is within the 'Edit Contact Details' section of your profile. Most people use LinkedIn®'s standard drop-down box which includes 'Personal Website', 'Company Website', 'Blog' etc. These are pretty boring descriptions and everyone uses them on LinkedIn®.

They do not really entice someone to want to click on the link though. There is a different way to add your website to any link and be able to include a 'Call to Action'. Instead of choosing 'Company Website' from the drop-down menu, choose 'Other'.

LinkedIn® will then give you a short space to write some text, and then a new place to add your link.

Here are some examples:

Old Description: Blog
New Description: Click for top Business Tips (link goes to your blog page)

Old Description: Company Website
New Description: For great value Hosting Packages (link goes to your products page)

Old Description: Personal Website
New Description: Get your FREE special report (link goes to a landing opt-in page)

Add a Phone Number and Email to your profile.

Make sure that you at least have an email address for business and a phone number for your office. From the LinkedIn® smartphone App people can make a call to you directly from within your LinkedIn® profile.

You can control all settings for your profile within Privacy and Settings, you will find this on a menu in the top right of LinkedIn®, click on your photograph on 'Me' and you can find your privacy settings there. I also recommend having this information in your 'About' section.

How can I help?

I run monthly 1-Day workshops called *'Get Your LinkedIn® Profile Sorted!'*

Due to my international reach and my mission to create £1billion in sales for my clients, these workshops are live streamed each month. People also attend in person in the room with me at my headquarters in Derby, East Midlands, UK.

Typically SMEs with an SSI of less than 50, come to my 1-day workshop frustrated that they just aren't getting enough leads, with no idea where their next sale is coming from.

Many are overwhelmed, trying to juggle everything in their business and they just can't seem to find the time to do everything. Others are trying to build their personal brand and position themselves as the 'go-to' expert in their field, but just don't know where to start.

If you have just read the last few chapters of this book and are still not sure on your exact target market or where to start when it comes to your LinkedIn® profile, then you would probably benefit from spending a full day with me.

You can book online at https://www.linkedinbound.co.uk/book/ to *'Get Your LinkedIn® Profile sorted!'.*

CHAPTER 3
Recommendations

Recommendations are all about credibility, they are social proof that you are good at what you do and that other people should also buy from you. The more recommendation you have on your profile the more chance that someone will decide to do business with you. The beauty of LinkedIn® recommendations is that everyone can see who has recommended you, so this MUST be a core part of your sales process.

If you are using LinkedIn® to generate leads or to build your personal brand to position you as a 'go-to' person in your industry or specialisation, then you need to pay attention to recommendations on your profile. As an absolute minimum you should be aiming for 10+ but to really drive inbound leads and have people coming to you, your aim should be to become the most recommended version of you on LinkedIn®.

At the time of writing this book, I have 188 LinkedIn® recommendations, it's not the most of any Social Selling expert globally, but certainly in the UK. I mention this on the first paragraph of my LinkedIn® profile to draw the reader's attention to my recommendations.

Potential clients can read great stories about how you have helped your existing clients on your LinkedIn® profile, so it's worth investing some time in getting the right kind of recommendations. Here are some tips on how you can build in recommendations to your sales process:

1. If you deliver workshops or training then include a question on the form "If you have enjoyed the workshop/training' would it be OK to request a LinkedIn® recommendation from you?". All those who say yes, you have permission to request a recommendation from. This is a great way to quickly build up the number of recommendations on your profile

2. If you speak on stages, then at the end of your presentation ask for LinkedIn® recommendations if they got value

3. Look at your case studies and testimonials on your website. These people have already recommended you, just not on LinkedIn®. Revisit these people and ask them to put the same text up on LinkedIn® as a recommendation

4. Every new review on other platforms can and should be turned into a LinkedIn® recommendation. We all know the importance of

reviews. As my good friend Gordon Burcham always says, "nobody buys the products on Amazon, they buy the reviews". Each time someone leaves you a Facebook review or a review on your Google my Business page, then ask that person to copy and paste it into LinkedIn® as a recommendation for you

The best way to build up your recommendations, is to GIVE them! Every time you give a recommendation you are helping another person, this giving activity is a great way to build relationships, motivate your network to want to help you back and build greater credibility. You are really taking your relationship building to the next level when you focus on recommending others, as it means that your level of trust with those people is high.

I try to give a recommendation at least once every 2-4 weeks, it's one of my favourite things to do, as the other person is rarely expecting it and it makes them feel amazing.

Think of 3 people right now, with whom you have done business, who you could give a recommendation to:

Name: _____

Company: _____

Name: _____

Company: _____

Name: _____

Company: _____

Now think of 3 people who you could ask to recommend you. I wouldn't normally suggest asking unless you know the person really well, or they have already recommended you elsewhere:

Name: _____

Company: _____

Name: _____

Company: _____

Name: _____

Company: _____

If you need some ideas on who you could recommend, I have compiled a list of ideas to help you below.

Give Recommendations to Suppliers

When you recommend a supplier to your business, you are in effect motivating that person to give you a better service, prioritising you over other contacts and helping them to know who to focus on. If a supplier is good at what they do and you go and give them a surprise recommendation, it is a very powerful way to give. This giving activity will result in your supplier going above and beyond, so when you need a new connection or if you ask for their help in getting into one of their customers, they are more inclined to do it because you have already helped their business.

It is a nice thing to do, giving a recommendation to a supplier, as you are building the relationship to take it from a client/supplier position to a position of 'let's see how we can help each other with introductions' etc. Your suppliers will often be in and out of companies that you would love to work with, so do not underestimate their network and the value it could be to you.

Give Recommendations to Clients

Recommending clients or people you have worked with in client companies, is a really powerful way to retain customers, keep them happy and go above and beyond. If you are recommending their company to others and you want to maintain that business and make yourself irreplaceable to the customer, then this is a great way to cement a relationship.

Your only goal with every customer is to make yourself so valuable to that organisation that, even if someone else came along offering another solution, they would not change because they have you and you look after them so well that it would be impossible for them to go elsewhere.

Recommendations are one tool you have at your disposal to build a strong relationship. From a LinkedIn® perspective, giving a recommendation to the company on their company page and an individual that you deal with on their personal page, would be a great activity to think about doing on a regular basis.

Give Recommendations to Colleagues

You can recommend people that you currently work with or people that you used to work with. We talked earlier about the value of connecting with old dormant contacts, giving them a recommendation is a sure way to get them to agree to meet with you for a coffee or lunch or over Skype (depending on your location), to have a catch up.

If you are a business owner then recognising an employee through a LinkedIn® recommendation is a great way to gain more engagement from that staff member, motivating them to do more, achieve more and get more results for your business.

Give Recommendations to People who Refer you

You probably already have a great deal of your incoming new business from word of mouth introductions, people who refer you on a regular basis, whether that be friends and family or your existing clients spreading the word about what you offer. Just think about how much business has come in to your company from a word of mouth situation in the last 12 months alone. What have you done to thank the person who gave you a referral? One of many options you have is to give them a recommendation on LinkedIn®.

Imagine how that person would feel if you, out of the blue, wrote a fantastic LinkedIn® recommendation for them, as a way to thank them for the referred business they have given you. The only impact that this can have is a positive one. Now they have been rewarded for an act of positivity, they are more likely to repeat that behaviour and refer you again because you thanked them through a recommendation.

Get Recommendations from those who Know, Like & Trust you

I have been asked so many times to give a recommendation on LinkedIn® to someone I either barely know or don't know at all. Essentially you should only be asking the connections you have on LinkedIn® for a recommendation if you have already built up a real business or personal relationship with them.

They have to know you, like you and trust you before they would even consider giving you a recommendation, so don't approach all of the LinkedIn® connections you have, be strategic, pick people who you know will say yes.

Get High Profile Recommendations

People don't just read what the recommendation says, they also look at who is giving the recommendation. Does it look better to have a bunch of recommendations from other small local business owners, or would it be better to have recommendations from a well-known brand?

If you do business with a well-known company, a high profile brand, then get a personal recommendation on LinkedIn® from the person you are dealing with. Large corporates very rarely provide testimonials or case studies, but in many cases they will allow their staff to give LinkedIn® recommendations.

The more senior the role the better, I love having C-Suite recommendations of companies I have impacted through social selling. Their recommendations carry a lot of weight and I use them in my marketing, on my website and in proposals to win more corporate clients.

Downloading Recommendations

I always recommend backing up your data on LinkedIn®, especially when you have as many connections and recommendations as I do. You can download your data in your privacy settings on LinkedIn®, which you can find in the menu called 'Me' in the top right-hand side of your homepage, in the desktop version of LinkedIn®.

How to Structure a great Recommendation

When you give a recommendation to another person, your name and business remains on that person's LinkedIn® profile, as long as they choose to show it, that's essentially free advertising space for you to showcase who you are and what you do. You never know who is going to be reading the recommendation that you write about someone else. So the VCO process comes in here too.

The structure I am about to give you, I learnt from my amazing mentor Marcus Cauchi. It can be used for LinkedIn® recommendations but also can apply to video testimonials, capturing of case studies etc.

This is a structure you can use to both give your own recommendations and to ask your clients to recommend you.

Question 1: Who are you and who do you help?

Question 2: What challenge(s) were you having before working with me?

Question 3: What reservations did you have before working with me?

Question 4: What surprised/delighted you?

Question 5: What results have you had since working with me?

Question 6: Why was it fun working with me?

Question 7: Would you recommend me and why?

Imagine you taking the time to answer all of these questions about a supplier or a client and the impact this would have on the recommendation quality. In the reverse how great is it to have your clients sharing this information about how you have helped them!

Most people, when you ask them to write a recommendation, won't know what to say and aren't comfortable writing. My suggestion is that you schedule a time to call them or meet, ask them these questions over the phone, type up the answers and then send it to them, already written in the form of a LinkedIn® recommendation. Ask them to check it's in line with what they said and then all they have to do is copy and paste into the recommendation.

How to Give/Request a LinkedIn® Recommendation

Firstly, to either give or receive a LinkedIn® recommendation you have to already be connected to the person on LinkedIn®, making you 1st degree connections.

Visit the person's profile that you are looking for by searching for their name.

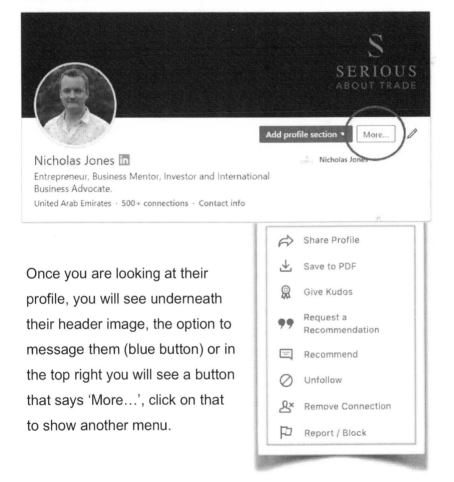

Once you are looking at their profile, you will see underneath their header image, the option to message them (blue button) or in the top right you will see a button that says 'More...', click on that to show another menu.

The new menu will appear with several options. The option to 'Request a Recommendation' or 'Recommend' is in the drop-down menu. When you choose either option, another screen will open. LinkedIn® is looking for you to share how you know each other and in which company you/they were working (depending on who is giving/receiving), to establish what role the recommendation is relevant to.

Just take note of the other options in this menu here as you may not have realised that you can save people's profiles to PDF and share their profile with a connection. It's also the menu you can use to unfollow someone's posts (but still stay connected), remove a connection and/or block a profile.

CHAPTER 4
Prospecting to Build your Pipeline

PART 1: Adding People You Already Know -Warm Market

Prospecting is one of the most important skills to develop if you are looking to build your sales pipeline and increase the number of new clients you are bringing into your business. It is so important that I have allocated two separate chapters to prospecting.

Part 1, this Chapter is all about adding people you already know to your LinkedIn® network. Part 2, Chapter 5 is all about adding people you don't know from your exact target market. Your approach on LinkedIn® with the people you already know from your existing network will be very different to prospecting those that you don't know.

Right now, no matter where you are in your career or business, you have both personal and business contacts that you have built up over time. Your network is completely unique to you, now it's time leverage it!

LinkedIn® works on the simple premise that we are all connected through six degrees of separation. This means that you can reach any contact no matter how famous through a maximum of six people in your network. LinkedIn® will show you all of your 1st, 2nd and 3rd degree connections. People beyond 3rd degree are not visible to you.

A common misconception with LinkedIn® is that when you add a new connection, you are just adding that one person. In actual fact you are adding them, plus their 1st and 2nd degree connections, into your network. Your existing network of contacts will quite often lead you to a dream client or someone you actually want to do business with.

Take me as an example. If before reading this book we were not connected to each other, just by adding Sam Rathling into your LinkedIn® network, you now have me as a 1st degree connection, plus my 16,000+ connections are now in your 2nd degree and their 1st degree connections are in your 3rd degree connections. You literally added hundreds of thousands into your network when you added me.

So if you ran a search for someone in your target market, they are more likely to show up, the larger your 1st degree network is. I will focus on finding people in your target market in the next chapter, I just want you to understand the power of your existing contacts.

For now, let's look at those people you already know. Think back to when you were age 13, and start there. Think about people you were at school with, friends you made, teachers, mentors, the parents of your friends, then college or university. Any work experience or internships that you completed. Now start looking at your career history, think about where you have worked previously, clients you used to work with, colleagues, bosses, managers.

What about suppliers, who have you bought from in the past, who serves you as a customer now? Think about neighbours past and present, what about voluntary or community work, charities you have been involved with. Now look to sports, hobbies, interests outside of work. How many contacts are there in your mobile phone?

Many of these people you will have lost contact with, others you may be connected with on other social media platforms such as Facebook. Each one on average has a network of 1000+ people, and many of them are in your network in the real world, but just aren't connected to you on LinkedIn® in your digital world. Imagine if they were!

How many more connections could you add to your network, just by looking at who you already know. How many of them know what you do now? How many could be a perfect client for you? My guess is that you are leaving money on the table by not exploring your existing networks.

Complete the table below with the total estimated number of contacts from each group of people. There may be some cross over, so when you total up the amount, take off 25% to give you an estimate of your overall network.

HOT CONTACTS	ESTIMATED NUMBER OF CONTACTS
Your Mobile Phone	
Facebook Personal Friends	
Facebook Fan Page Followers	
School Friends	
College Friends	
University Friends	
Ex-Colleagues	
Twitter Followers	
Spouse/Partners Network	
Neighbours Past & Present	
Workplace Contacts	
Community Contacts	
Sports/Interests/Hobbies Contacts	
Networking Groups Contacts	
Clients - Current & Past	
Suppliers - Current & Past	
Existing LinkedIn Contacts (1st Connections)	
Friends and Friends of Friends	
Family (Close & Extended)	
Existing Mailing List of Contacts (CRM system)	
Business Cards on your desk and in your drawers	
TOTAL NUMBER CONTACTS:	

Now, go to LinkedIn® and click on the people icon 'My Network' to show how many LinkedIn® connections you have today. There is likely to be a big difference between the number of contacts you know and those you have on LinkedIn®. What a massive opportunity!

If you have less than 500 connections at the time of reading this book, start with building up your network on LinkedIn® with the people you already know. Add 10 people a day from your existing network, work on the basis that 70% will accept. Within 10 weeks you will have built up a solid network of new connections. This activity will lead you to conversations with people you may not have had contact with for a long time, which could lead to sales opportunities.

When we start to look at prospecting in your target market in the next Chapter, you will see much better results from your advanced searching by establishing this broad base on connections first.

Here are a few of the suggested groups of people that I recommend adding as a priority:

Connect with Ex-Colleagues

These are quite often dormant connections, people who you may not have dealt with in a number of years. They will have a strong affinity with you, will want to help you and since you were last in contact will have been advancing their career and building an amazing network themselves, which could be of use to you and vice versa. It is always worthwhile touching base with ex-colleagues.

A quick story to demonstrate this, a business coach in the UK, Andrew came on one of my LinkedIn® Masterclasses back in 2011. We talked about the benefits of connecting with people you used to work with, including ex-colleagues, team members, managers and subordinates.

After that Masterclass he reconnected with an ex-colleague of 15 years previous, they had worked together at Unilever. That one re-connection he made transformed his business and in 2012, that re-established relationship was worth 75% of his turnover that year. She had since become a senior board level executive in another FMCG company and when they reconnected, Andrew's business provided the exact services that she was looking for.

LinkedIn® is very intuitive and provides a great way to connect with people you have previously worked with called 'People you May Know'. This will never run out of options and uses the data you enter into your work experience section of your profile to determine ex-colleagues you might know based on where you have previously worked. So be sure to update the work history in your LinkedIn® profile to get an accurate suggestions list from LinkedIn® within the 'People you may Know' area.

Connect with Clients

One of the easiest ways to build your 1st degree connections is to connect with all of your current and previous clients. Even if you have not done business with someone for a while, it's a good way to re-engage with them and re-kindle the relationship. Remember you cannot be recommended by a client, unless they are a 1st degree connection. Add your current and past clients on LinkedIn®, and then support their posts, follow their content and stay engaged with what they are doing.

Connect with your Staff

If you run a business with a team, then ensure that you connect with each of your staff. Ensure that you have a solid social media policy in place, then train your entire team how to use LinkedIn® and social selling effectively. Imagine the impact you could make across LinkedIn®, by each one of your team building brand awareness of your company, increasing the amount of 1st degree connections and prospecting daily in your target market. Each of your team bring a different background, education, work history and you never know who they know, who they have in their network. Connect with them, give them Kudos publicly and recommend them to build relationships and make them feel valued.

Connect with Friends & Family

Connecting with friends and family can sometimes reveal some interesting facts about people who you have known for years, especially your extended family. Connect with your parents, grandparents, sisters, brothers, uncles, aunts, cousins and you just never know what opportunities are going to come up.

At most family gatherings you are completely focused on the family, children, personal things, but imagine coming back into a work environment to discover that one of your close family members actually knows the person you have been trying to land as a client for weeks. It is an obvious one, but not everyone does this. You just might be surprised!

Connect with Old School, College & University Friends

You never know where your past colleagues are now working, you also don't know who they know. It can be so much fun going back over the old college year books and into the Alumni groups on LinkedIn® to find people who you used to hang out with at School, College or University. Every university has a page on LinkedIn® and you can use LinkedIn® to identify these people.

Find the university that you went to school in, and on the right hand-side menu choose 'Alumni'. Now enter the years that you attended and hit enter and a list of all people who were at that university at the same time as you will show up. You can then run searches within this. This is such a powerful way to build up your connections. Some will be running their own business now, some will be climbing the career ladder in large companies, you just never know where they are and how you can help them and vice versa.

Connect with Suppliers

Your supplier's networks are invaluable. As a customer of their business, if you asked for help in securing a connection or help in supporting your posts, I am sure that they would be happy to help. They want to keep you as a customer and are more than likely to connect with you and more importantly, facilitate introductions to other people in their network.

Connect with the Business Cards on your Desk

I am sure, if you are like most business owners, that you have a stack of business cards either on your desk or hidden in a drawer or a box somewhere. Each of these business cards represents someone you have once met and exchanged cards with. By connecting with each of these people you are creating another touch point with these contacts and may rekindle some business relationships that you had not kept up to date with. Just by adding each person whose business card you are holding on to you could add significant connections to your total LinkedIn® network.

Connect with Neighbours

When I say neighbours, there are two types. Those you live near or next to and those you work near or next to. Look outside the building where you work, in many cases you will be surrounded by other companies. Find them on LinkedIn® and add them to your network. You probably already say hello to each other in the car park or around the building you share so add them to your LinkedIn® network. Do the same with the people you share the same street with.

5 Actionable Insights

1. Personalise every connection request to each person, with how you know each other.

2. Add 10 connections per day to build up your 1st degree connections.

3. Start conversations by asking questions, find out what they have been up to.

4. See how you can help each other.

5. Have fun! This is a simple and fun exercise that should not be neglected.

So before you start tackling the world of cold market prospecting with people you don't know (coming up in the next Chapter), think about how much money you are leaving on the table by not having the people you already know in your network.

CHAPTER 5
Prospecting to Build your Pipeline
PART 2: Adding People You Don't Know - Cold Market

Regardless of the number of connections you have today, your LinkedIn® network is going to do one thing consistently and that is, grow. Even if you are purely reactive on LinkedIn®, you will receive connection requests and this in turn will increase the number of people in your network. If you really want to benefit from LinkedIn® and social selling, it is important that you understand how to search for people and companies in your exact target market.

The most common question I get asked is "Should I connect with people I don't know?". I do recommend that (within reason) you accept each connection request that you receive. Even though you don't know the person directly, their LinkedIn® network could lead you to a massive contract or could offer up a dream 2nd or 3rd connection that you would never have been able to see before. Check their profile, look at their photograph and network size, see if they are posting regularly and read what they say in their connection request.

Always bear in mind that LinkedIn® is a professional, business networking platform and most people treat it that way. You never know why someone you don't know is asking for you to connect with them. It could just be that they want to do business with you, having read your amazing profile or been referred to you.

Imagine that you are at a networking event or function, someone coming over to you that you don't know, they reach out their hand to introduce themselves and you just walk away, and ignore them. You didn't know who they were, who they know or why they wanted to come over and introduce themselves. You could have just missed the chance to build a new relationship, get to know someone who could refer you to their network, or even worse, they could have been your next best client. This is effectively what you are doing.

You can always remove the new connection from your contacts if you don't like their approach, or unfollow them if their content is not for you. Bear in mind that most people on LinkedIn® are business professionals, just because you connect with someone you don't know today, it does not mean that they can do anything to you or your business, the more connections you have the more useful your LinkedIn® network can be to you.

The decision around whether you connect to people on LinkedIn® who you do not know is of course personal choice, just bear in mind all of the benefits that go with having a strong and large network before making the choice to restrict your network to people you know personally. It is also very easy to block, report or remove a connection that you accept and no longer want to have in your network.

Ideally you want to be aiming for at least 1000 1st degree connections on LinkedIn®, this is where you will start to gain traction, your content will reach more people and you are increasing the chance of your exact target market showing up in search results.

This chapter will help you with advanced searching techniques to tap into your LinkedIn® network, using one of my favourite social selling tactics, Boolean search.

Boolean Search

Boolean search is an advanced way of searching data and, when you apply it within LinkedIn®, you will dramatically improve your search results. It will help you to organise your keywords and secure you better, more targeted results.

Most people use a very basic search on LinkedIn®, they head to the search bar at the top of the screen, then type in random keywords, job titles and hope for the best. They then get frustrated as thousands of results show up, many of which are not exactly what they were looking for. Before they know it, LinkedIn® is putting restrictions on them for running too many searches as they have hit their 'Commercial Search Limit'. Any of this sound familiar?

Boolean can look and sound very complex, but it really isn't. Boolean search is using specific logic using just 5 key operators to help you get more targeted results when you search.

The 5 elements of syntax are:

- OR
- AND
- NOT
- " " (quotation marks)
- ( ) brackets

I will go through each one in detail below and then give you some examples of each one in action. Then we can look at your own target market and give you some relevant Boolean searches for you to use and apply within LinkedIn®.

The OR Syntax

OR provides you with options in your search. Usage of the OR command (which must be written in CAPS) allows you to create a list of possibilities for which only one match is important.

For example, the following Boolean string search phrase would give you results that contain one or more of the stated words:

Director OR Partner OR Owner

The AND Syntax

AND is the simplest function to apply. Any search terms that follow an AND operator must appear in the results. For example:

Landlord AND "Property Investment"

will give results that include both the word "Landlord" and the phrase "Property Investment". All search results will include both.

The NOT Syntax

NOT is the command of exclusion. If there are any closely related terms that mean very different things, then usage of the NOT command is extremely valuable. An example could be as follows:

Landlord NOT Pub

This would give you results that contain the word Landlord, but leaving out any that use the Pub. Very useful if you are targeting property Landlords and you don't want your search results to be full of people who run pubs.

The one major limitation with the NOT command is that it is not recognised by Google, but it will work on your LinkedIn® searches.

The Use of "" Quotation Marks

You probably noticed that I used the " " expression above in an example already, wrapped around particular keywords. These quotation marks are used to capture a full phrase that is to be kept intact, in the precise word order stated. Not using ""quotation marks around a phrase will mean that each word is treated separately, usually with an assumed AND in between each one. For example:

Managing Director

would give results that contain 'managing' and 'director', but not necessarily in the same sentence or paragraph. So if you are prospecting for Managing Directors, then your search results are going to show up with all the LinkedIn® profiles containing the word 'managing' and all of the LinkedIn® profiles with the word 'director' leading you to thousands of irrelevant search results and a list of the wrong people.

"Managing Director"

would give results that only contain the exact phrase "Managing Director". This can be applied to any specific phrase. If you were prospecting business owners, they may have a whole range of job titles. So you would want to be focused on the right phrases and wrapping them with quotation marks.

"Managing Director" OR "Business Owner"

The Use of ( ) Brackets

Using brackets is absolutely essential for complex search strings, and it can be the application of brackets that causes the most confusion. Essentially, a clause within brackets is given priority over other elements around it.

The most common place that brackets are applied by advanced users of Boolean is in the use of OR strings. Perhaps a good example would be a series of job titles where you also need to have a specific keyword on their LinkedIn® Profile.

("Managing Director" OR "MD" OR "Business Owner" OR "Founder") AND ("Start Up" OR "Scale Up")

To combine both commands into one Boolean search, you can use brackets to tell LinkedIn® that these are separate conditions. It makes no difference which order the two bracketed sections go; the same results will result either way.

Who invented Boolean?

George Boole invented Boolean logic over 200 years ago. He was a largely self-taught English mathematician, philosopher and logician. His work on logic laid many of the foundations for the digital revolution. His legacy was Boolean logic, a theory of mathematics in which all variables are either "true" or "false", or "on" or "off". This logic still underpins all digital devices, existing in almost every line of computer code, and it just so happens to be the means by which recruiters and sales professionals search for prospects and candidates on LinkedIn® (and other platforms) today.

There are, of course, several other Boolean modifiers you can use to further refine and improve your Boolean searches, as well as many more rules for the use of Boolean in various other search engines and databases beyond LinkedIn®.

Applying Boolean within LinkedIn® to Find your Exact Target Market

For this you will need to revisit the work that we did in the introduction section of this book on your target market. You wrote down some job titles and industry sectors as well as locations where you want to find potential clients.

Using the Boolean logic that I just gave you, come up with some Boolean search strings below to help you with searching on LinkedIn®.

Once you have written these down, you simply type the full string into the search bar on LinkedIn® (on the free version) or the search bar in Sales Navigator if you hold a licence for that.

A simple OR Search using job titles:

_____ OR _____

OR _____ OR _____

An OR search in combination with a keyword or key phrase:

(_____ OR _____ OR

_____ OR _____) AND

_____

Remember to put phrases in "quotation marks" to ensure you get specific results.

I usually spend a couple of hours practising this technique, prospecting with people who attend my Masterclass as it can take some time to get used to running complex Boolean searches and then using LinkedIn's filters to refine the searches. Practice, practice, practice is what you need to get better and more targeted results.

Once you have run a couple of Boolean searches, use the filters that LinkedIn® provides at the top of the screen (on the free version) and on the left hand-side (on Sales Navigator) to then filter your list to include industry sectors, locations etc.

I do recommend prospecting for people in your target market in your 2nd degree network only. These people share mutual connections with you already, you have some common ground and it's slightly more warmed up. You can add this filter in to your searches and only choose to see those people at 2nd degree.

Once you have 1000+ connections in your network your 2nd degree network will get bigger and have more results.

When you first start out you may find this limits how many people you can see in your exact target market, but if you run the exact same Boolean search in a month from now your results will be massively different if you are prospecting every day. Be consistent and focus on the activity of prospecting daily, not the results, they will come over time.

Personalise your Connection Requests

My recommendation is that when you add a new connection, that you ALWAYS personalise the message to them. Use their first name and customise the message based on something in their profile. The purpose of this first message is simply to get the person to accept your request and connect with you. Nothing else!

There should never be any sales pitch or sales related language in your first message. One objective only, that they click 'Accept'. There is nothing worse than someone trying to sell in the first message. If you approach your prospecting in the right way you should achieve a conversion of 50-80%. i.e. that if you send out 10 connection requests a day, that 5-8 will accept. If your conversion rate is very low, either your targeting is all wrong or your message is too 'salesy'.

Keep it simple, you only have 295 characters to write a first message. Keep it informal, use first names for you and them. And use language that is appropriate to their level of seniority. The way you write to a local start-up business owner will be different to the way you approach a CEO of a multinational company.

Always find common ground, whether it be the connections you have in common, shared interests, same university or a sports team. Look at their profile to find something that you can relate to them with.

Look at how other people connect with you. What do you like? What phrases do other people use when adding you that compels you to accept? At the same time, look at what turns you off, what phrases and connection messages don't you like.

It's important to be authentically you, use your voice. You have to stand out but not sell. I have a number of template messages that I use for a 2nd degree connection request, but they are all different because a Sales Director with a team of 100 needs a different approach to a local business owner who may want to come on a workshop with me.

The main thing is to never, ever, ever SELL!

89

Commercial Search Limit

I mentioned LinkedIn®'s commercial search limit earlier. If you are on the free version of LinkedIn® and you go from not searching much, to prospecting daily as a result of reading this book, you may run into something called the 'commercial search limit'. This is a restriction that LinkedIn® brings into play when you have performed too many searches.

Boolean string searches will help you somewhat, as you are effectively searching for 4 or 5 job titles in one string, but I am warning you now that this may happen to you. LinkedIn® uses this as a way to get you to upgrade to Premium and Sales Navigator products (more on these later in Chapter 11). If you hit your commercial search limit, LinkedIn® will offer you a free trial of their other products.

There is not a standard or exact number of searches per month and it is different for every person's LinkedIn® account. Bear in mind that every time you put anything into the search bar, even if it is a person's name or a company name, you are using up a search.

The more active you become in searching and prospecting, the higher chance that LinkedIn® will flag your account as a prospect for their paid products. So my message here is, don't go crazy, be sensible with your Boolean searches and later in the book I will share more about Premium and Sales Navigator so you can make an informed decision about what is right for you.

If you do hit the commercial search limit then you will need to wait until the 1st of the next calendar month for this to be released and for you to be able to search again. LinkedIn® provides us all with an amazing tool for networking and building relationships and growing our personal and professional brand. They have to make money and this is one tool they use to grow their business.

Be aware of it, respect the limits and use your Boolean strings to reduce the chances of it happening to you.

They Accepted! What Next?

Great job! You have run your Boolean search, filtered your list and chosen who you want to proactively add into your network and they accepted! Now what?

Now that these targeted people are in your network, they will get to see your amazing content, specifically aimed at them (more on that in Chapter 6). You are growing your network with people who fit your exact target market. You sound them, selected them and approached them, but what does it mean?

Well, you are now 1st degree connections, which means that you can message your new connection directly with no restriction from LinkedIn®. However, the mistake that most make people on

LinkedIn® i.e. the ones who don't understand social selling, is that they take this opportunity to land a long sales pitch all about them into the new connection's inbox. It usually happens within a matter of seconds of the connection request being accepted. Yuck! I get these daily and I am sure you have experienced this too. Don't do it… just don't. It repels your potential clients, you will get blocked and possibly reported to LinkedIn® for spamming and selling.

So let's look at the right way to approach your follow up. It is this, your second message, that will make all the difference to your social selling success. Your second message needs to focus on the prospective client, it needs to be all about them and it needs to start a conversation.

"Conversation is the new lead" Ryan Deiss, Digital Marketer

This is one of my favourite social selling quotes. It's not about selling, it's about starting a real human to human (H2H) conversation with the person who is behind that LinkedIn® profile. One of the best ways to do this is to ask a question. When you ask a strong question you will start a conversation. This is especially true if when you reach out to them, they are already talking about their problem internally.

Here is an example connection follow up message that I use with Sales Directors in companies with a turnover of more than £10m with sales teams of 20+ salespeople.

Hi Tim,

Many thanks for accepting my connection request.

Typically Sales Directors come to me, concerned that they have invested heavily in LinkedIn® Sales Navigator yet their salespeople are still not generating enough leads.

Some are worried about missing targets and are under pressure from key stakeholders to get results. A few know that they should be generating more business from LinkedIn® but just don't know how to unlock its potential with their team.

I don't suppose any of that sounds familiar?

Out of interest, what % of your team's sales revenue is coming from LinkedIn®?

Sam

Now not every Sales Director or Commercial Director that I send this message to, is going to respond, but at the time of writing this I generate a 5-10% response rate to this message. I really don't care what the answer is to the question.

Why? Because any response to this question, gives me an opportunity to move this conversation from the online to the offline:

- If they are generating zero business from LinkedIn® - I can help

- If they have no clue what % is coming from LinkedIn® - I can help

- Whether he responds with 5% or 25% or higher I know I can help increase it

Let's say I send this message to a frustrated Sales Director who is under pressure and not hitting their targets, I will have hit a pain point. In most cases they want to solve it. The most important part about this message is that I have given them a question that is simple to answer, makes them think and encourages a reply.

I have not pitched my services or tried to sell him anything. All I have done is attempt to start a conversation. As soon as he replies I know I can move them to a phone call or a meeting.

How could you apply this in your own business? Come up with your version of a follow up second message.

I recommend sending out your follow up messages within 24-48 hours of your new connections accepting your connection request, certainly not immediately! Make this a part of your weekly activities, keep a track of your conversion rates and maybe test a few different versions to see which gives you the best response rate. It took me months to nail the right message for prospecting in my three different target markets. Be patient.

When I craft these messages personally for the clients who choose to outsource their LinkedIn® prospecting to us, I will usually take at least 1-2 hours coming up with different versions for them. We don't always get it right straight away but when we do it's like tapping into a vein and the conversations start flowing.

To learn more about accelerating your LinkedIn® lead generation, send me a message on LinkedIn® or email: hello@LinkedInbound.co.uk.

Building your Network with People You Don't Know

Connect with Thought Leaders in your Industry

Regardless of the industry you are in, there will be key players globally who speak and write in your industry. You can typically find these people by researching your topic on the internet. TED talks are a great place to find Thought Leaders, you can brush their ego when approaching these people, when you ask them to connect mention how much you were inspired by their talk, their presentation or what they said.

People who write in well-known publications, those you read about and people who are on stages at industry events and conferences you attend, are great people to add into your network. Look at people who are publishing articles on LinkedIn®

about your specialist area, or those who are blogging / vlogging about your niche or industry.

Think about the podcasts that you enjoy listening to and the books that you have read.

Authors, Podcast hosts and guests will appreciate you connecting with them. In many cases, because these people are considered 'thought leaders' you will notice that their LinkedIn® 1st degree networks will be 10,000+ and this will help to build your 2nd degree connections.

I often have people connecting with me because I have made an impact on them on a podcast interview or Facebook Live or a webinar I have appeared on. I love being connected to those who enjoy what I do. It will be the same for others who share their expertise. Expect a positive response as long as your approach is about them and mentions why you were inspired to connect with them.

If you are reading this book, then you are most likely to be interested in improving your business in some way. I absolutely love reading books, especially listening to them on Audible. I always add the Author to my LinkedIn® network when I love their book. You'll be surprised, people who write books genuinely want to be in touch with their followers and will usually connect with a fan. Have a practice now.

Connect with Sam Rathling here:

https://www.linkedin.com/in/samrathling-linkedinexpert

Just mention in your message that you are reading this book! I will gladly connect with you and that way you can continue to learn from me on your LinkedIn® journey.

Connect with Referral Partners

Find people in professions or categories that you know you would be able to give referrals to if you built up a strong relationship. Below are some examples of the kind of Referral Partners or Introducers for various industries:

Profession:	Good Referral Partners:
Photographer	Jeweller, Travel Agent, Videographer, Bridal Shop, Wedding Planner
Plumber	Builder, Electrician, Roofer, Plasterer, Architect, Engineer
Recruitment	Human Resources Consultant, Business Coach, Accountant, Printer, Training Company
Accountant	Solicitor, Financial Advisor, Bank Manager, Business Coach, Sales Trainer
Web Designer	Copywriter, Marketing, Graphic Designer, Printer, Promotional Products

Think about what type of referral partners would be right for your business. Then start researching these using LinkedIn®.

Apply the same search techniques that we have already talked about earlier in this chapter and use the keywords and key phrases to find them. Then narrow and refine your search to your locality and you'll start to find good people to partner with to help you reach multiple end clients.

Company Searches to find Your Target Market

So far in this chapter we have focused on finding your target market through people searches. But what if you already know which company you want to work with. How can you use the same methods to find the name of the person you want to speak to?

Having a Top 50 or Top 100 dream client list is a great idea, the challenge is then finding the right decision maker within those companies. When cold calling you will hit gatekeepers, people who are employed to let only the right calls through. The great thing about LinkedIn® is that you can get directly into a decision makers inbox, where there is a lot less noise than their email inbox. On average, a senior manager in a large company will receive 140 emails a day, on LinkedIn® it will be less than 10 per day. I know which inbox I would rather be competing in!

Start by entering the Company name into the search bar, choose the right company from the list (some large enterprise accounts will have multiple company pages by country or industry sector). When you arrive onto their Company page, you will see a header image and on the right-hand side underneath the company header image there will be a blue link with the total number of employees on LinkedIn®. Click that to pull up a list of all employees who currently work for that organisation.

Once again, the filters will appear at the top of the screen on the free version and on the left hand-side for those of you using Sales Navigator. If you choose 'All Filters' on the free version of LinkedIn® you have the option to run a Boolean search on job titles or departments. Be aware that not all of them will be in your 2nd degree network, some will be harder to reach than others. Connect at multiple layers within the organisation, both junior level and senior level as this will open up more 2nd degree connections for you.

The ability to find out a decision makers name gives you a competitive edge, and nothing beats picking up the phone! If your LinkedIn® approach doesn't hit the mark, then you can call knowing the name of the person you want to speak to.

Back Up Your Connections by Exporting Data from LinkedIn®

What would you do if you lost your LinkedIn® account? It is vital that you understand the LinkedIn® https://www.LinkedIn.com/legal/user-agreement and guidelines. You could violate the user agreement and instantly lose access to your LinkedIn® account. I know people who have had this

99

happen to them, one marketing consultant I know, was generating 50% of her revenue from LinkedIn® and just like that it was taken away. Unfortunately, she had not backed up her data and lost access to LinkedIn® for over 6 months and her revenues plummeted.

At any stage you could lose your LinkedIn® account so my advice is always keep it backed up. You can back up your data from within your *'Privacy & Settings'* within LinkedIn®. There is a section called *'How LinkedIn® Uses your Data'* within the Privacy tab, and then you can click on *'Download my Data'*.

You have two choices here, a) The Works or b) Pick and Choose. If you have never downloaded your data before, I recommend choosing *'The Works'*. It will take about 24 hours to complete and LinkedIn® will send you a zip file of everything you have ever done on LinkedIn® in, including articles, recommendations, posts, your connections etc. If you ever lost your LinkedIn® account at least you have a backup of your network and the historical activity.

If you choose one item, such as *'Connections'* it will take a maximum of 10 minutes and you will then have a full back up of your 1st degree connections. The data is simple, it contains their name, job title, company and in some cases an email but 95% of emails are blocked since GDPR came into play.

Use this data for your own records, if you have a CRM system you could upload them there and flag them as LinkedIn® 1st degree connections, but they should not to be added to any mailing lists or newsletters because these people have not opted in to receive emails from you.

All zip files, regardless of what you choose to download will be emailed to the email account that you use to login to LinkedIn®. You will also need your password to be able to trigger the download.

You will be able to access the file from within the Privacy settings as well as on email. They download as CSV files, which you can open within Excel.

I find the 'My Network' area, where you can see all of your connections, quite difficult to navigate now that I have over 15,000 connections, so having access to them all on a spreadsheet gives me greater visibility on my network and allows me to navigate my network more easily.

Back up, back up, back up…

You have invested time and energy in building up your LinkedIn® network, visibility and credibility, don't lose it!

5 Actionable Insights:

1. Personalise every connection request, even if you don't know them

2. Add 10 connections per day, that you don't know, to build up your 1st degree connections with people in your exact target market. Expect 50-70% to accept

3. Use Boolean search to get more targeted results. Write your Boolean searches down and try a variety of different searches to give you prospect lists in your exact target market

4. Test a variety of 2nd messages with great questions to check your conversion rates, into positive conversations

5. Back up your connections every month

CHAPTER 6
Prospecting to Gain Competitive Edge

There are some key things you can do, to set yourself apart from your competition. LinkedIn® has some amazing features that so few people know about, you can really stand out from the crowd and cut through all the noise in the inbox of your potential clients and your existing connections.

Prospect Daily

You picked up this book to learn how to generate leads on LinkedIn®. Prospecting is one of the most important elements to success on LinkedIn®. Prospecting every day, building up your connections in your target market is critical to you generating leads. I can say with certainty that your competition won't be doing this, certainly not daily and it's unlikely that they will be prospecting consistently. I see hundreds of salespeople and business owners each month and when I ask this question, it is staggering how few are prospecting. This is one way to gain competitive advantage.

Being proactive, adding new people daily who match your exact target market, will start conversations with the right people, meaning that people you actually want to do business with will see your amazing content (more on that in Chapter 7), plus you will get into the habit of building your sales pipeline for the long term. I recommend that you add a minimum of 10 connections a day in your target market. This will take you less than 10 minutes (once you get better at Boolean and more practiced in prospecting). Run your Boolean search, filter using the filters LinkedIn® provides, go through the list and choose 10 profiles of people to invite into your network.

If you are a small business owner or micro-business, it is vital that you prospect daily, even if you are super busy. If you don't you may end up in a rollercoaster cycle of winning business, getting busy, delivering the work and then coming to the end of a project and realising you don't know where the next one is coming from. If you are in sales, you I am sure will want to smash your sales targets and hit your commission bonuses; this will only happen if you have a full pipeline. Prospecting daily on LinkedIn® should be a part of your daily habits, especially if you have LinkedIn® Sales Navigator (covered in Chapter 11).

Prospecting in Technicolour

LinkedIn® has recently introduced some amazing features to messaging. You can now send any of the following to a connection from within your LinkedIn® inbox once someone becomes a 1st degree connection:

- An attachment
- An image taken directly from your Camera
- A video message
- An image from your picture gallery/album
- A GIF
- Your Location
- Your availability (links to your Calendar)

Want to stand out from the crowd and cut through the noise? Send someone a video message or a voice message. Using media to respond to messages and when prospecting can give you an edge and set you apart from all of the other messages your prospects are receiving in their LinkedIn® inbox.

Voice messages are restricted to 60 seconds (I would recommend about 30 seconds or less to have the most impact. You can choose to 'cancel' or 'send' when you record a voice message, in case you make a mistake you can re-record. Get comfortable with voice and always remember, no selling or pitching! Same VCO rules apply.

If you are sending a video, then I recommend recording it with captions, using an app like Clip-O-Matic (more on this in Chapter 7).

More than 85% of LinkedIn® users will watch or read video without sound. So include captions if you are sending a video message.

I absolutely love that you can record an audio message or send a video. It's so much more personal, you can bring in tonality and personality and increase the chances of your message being heard by your prospect or new connection. Most people on LinkedIn® are not even aware that you can use voice and video so when they receive one, they become curious and often have fun responding in the same way. You are probably already using voice and video on Whatsapp, messenger and other forms of social media. So start prospecting in technicolour, have fun, be brave and go for it!

Using LinkedIn® for Research

LinkedIn® is a phenomenal research tool. You can learn so much about a potential prospect just by doing some simple research on both them and the company they work for, which will increase the chances of you securing the business.

Researching the Individual

ACTION: Pick someone you are due to meet, someone you are prospecting or a new connection that is directly in your target market.

Now visit their profile on LinkedIn® and then answer these questions about them:

- How many mutual connections do you share?

- How many LinkedIn® Followers do they have?

- Which School, College or University did they attend?

- What education level did they achieve?

- Where are they based?

- Where have they previously worked? How long were they there?

- What Interests do they have?

- What groups do they belong to?

- What Influencers do they follow?

- What Companies do they follow?

- What types of content do they share?

- Who has recommended them?

- What voluntary causes or charities do they support?

Researching the Company

Now go to their current company, usually you can find this in the 'Work Experience' section of their LinkedIn® profile. Click on the logo next to their job title, now answer these questions about the Company:

- Which Company do they represent?

- How many employees does the Company have?

- What Competitors are identified in the company's 'Also Viewed' section

- Are they hiring? If so, what roles are they advertising?

- If you have a premium or Sales Navigator account, go to 'Insights' for details of hiring trends and what departments are in growth or decline

- What type of content and posts are they putting out on their Company page?

- How many followers does the Company Page have?

- What key Products and Services do they highlight in their Company page?

Imagine being armed with all this information before a meeting? LinkedIn® gives you so much information, and this can be one of the best ways to build rapport in the early stages of a new business relationship. Use this research to find out what you have in common, look at topics you could bring into the conversation. It takes some time to do this properly, but it's well worth it especially when you combine it with the next section of this Chapter, being able to know their personality profile.

Crystal Knows

This is my most favourite Chrome extension, I absolutely love it! Crystal Knows can tell you anyone's personality directly from their LinkedIn® Profile. It can help you to understand yourself better and improve your team, as well as prospect more effectively and close more deals.

Imagine going into a phone call or a sales meeting with a prospect, a decision maker you have never met before and actually understanding what makes them tick, how to speak with them, what to prepare and how to behave with them based on their detailed personality profile.

Welcome to Crystal Knows! You can visit their website and download the Chrome extension directly. There is also a mobile app version for using Crystal on the go. Get Crystal Knows Here. I share this amazing tool at my LinkedIn® Masterclasses and the amount of people who use it and then close deals because of their new found knowledge about their prospects, is astounding.

The free version gives you just 10 profiles in total, then you need to move to a premium account which is currently $29 per month on a recurring monthly subscription. In my opinion this is an

109

absolute bargain if you are in sales and choose to use it for each sales call or meeting.

How does it work?

Crystal analyses millions of data points to accurately identify anyone's personality. Crystal uses personality AI to accurately identify anyone's behavioural patterns by analysing text samples, assessment responses, and other attributes. As of July 2019, Crystal profiles are 80% accurate. I always recommend using Crystal as a guideline and this will give you significant competitive advantage for closing more sales.

5 Actionable Insights:

1. Prospect every single day, make the time to prospect and fill your pipeline.

2. Use LinkedIn® to research information about each prospect you are going to sell to.

3. Use LinkedIn® to research company information to give you different insights.

4. Stand out from the crowd by prospecting in technicolour using voice and video.

5. Apply the insights from Crystal to identify the personality type of your prospects

CHAPTER 7
Posting with Purpose

So far in this book I have covered many ways in which you can engage in conversation with your target market, which will lead to sales opportunities. These are proactive tactics where you can generate leads in a mostly outbound way, through LinkedIn® outreach and leveraging your new amazing LinkedIn® profile. Let's call this 'outbound lead generation'.

Now it's time to look at 'inbound lead generation'. Over the coming months and years, by applying the social selling strategies outlined in this book, you will be building up an incredible network of connections in your exact target market.

This chapter is all about content creation, posting with purpose. Helping you to leverage the LinkedIn® newsfeed to explode your visibility and credibility in ways that you have never done before. When you get your content marketing right, you can build your personal brand, connect with your audience and get your LinkedIn® network to know, like and trust you.

Content is King

If you aren't posting content on LinkedIn®, you may as well be invisible. Content helps you to position yourself as an expert in what you do (more on that in Chapter 8). If you do post content well and with a focus on your exact target market you will start to become known in your sector, and you will grow your connections and develop 'know, like and trust' of your personal brand. Everyone has heard the expression that 'Content is King', it absolutely is one of the best social selling strategies to drive inbound leads to your inbox on LinkedIn®. Almost every time I post on LinkedIn®, I get people sending me messages asking me how they can work with me. Approximately 400 inbound leads a month come into our business now as a result of social selling.

I set aside half a day a week for content creation, I am serious about being a dominant player globally and in order to achieve my big mission to create £1billion in sales for my clients, I have to be putting out great content to help my audience to become better at social selling through LinkedIn®. This does not mean you need to spend that much time on content, but you do need to be planning it out and thinking about what kind of content you could create to build your company brand (more on that in Chapter 9) and your personal brand through the LinkedIn® newsfeed.

Connection is Queen

Content may be King, but it is not purely about quantity of content, it also needs to connect with your audience. I say connection is Queen. Always keep your target market top of mind when posting on LinkedIn®. Remember, your LinkedIn® profile is aimed at your target market, you are prospecting to build up your network of connections in your target market, now you have to serve them with content that will educate, inspire and engage them. Over time as you build that connection with your audience, more of them will be attracted towards you, which will drive inbound leads.

The key factor here is authenticity. Be you, don't try to be anyone else. You are never going to connect with every single part of your network, you will draw the people towards you and attract the people who you connect with, and who will????see you for who you really are. Real is the new fake. The more raw and authentic your videos are the better. You don't need a big production crew, it does not need to be perfect. You are human, you will make mistakes. If you are recording a video, don't do 50 takes to get it perfectly right, go with the one that will connect best with your audience.

Engagement is Critical

Ever wondered why some of your posts receive hundreds or even thousands of views and others just simply fade into non-existence like tumbleweed? Well, this is all to do with how much engagement your post receives. Early engagement on a post, particularly in the first hour of a post going up will determine the momentum of that posts penetration into your LinkedIn® network. When you first put out a new piece of content on LinkedIn®, only 2% of your network see that post.

In order for the LinkedIn® algorithm to kick into gear and start sharing that content with more and more people in your network, the post needs to have lots of engagement. This means any of the 5 types of LinkedIn® reactions to the post, quite a new feature but a post can now receive a *'Like'*, a *'Love'*, a *'Celebrate'*, an *'Insightful'* or a *'Curious'* reaction. People can *'Share'* your post with their network, or they can *'Comment'* underneath the post. Preferably you want them to do all three or a combination of these responses.

LinkedIn® loves comments, in fact it weights these the highest. So if you post receives a significant amount of comments then more and more people will be exposed to that piece of content. Each comment can be commented back on, so ensure that when you receive a comment, that you respond by asking a question or driving discussion. Comments upon comments will help to drive engagement.

Some key things to bear in mind when it comes to LinkedIn® content creation, to maximise engagement:

- LinkedIn® wants you to create your own, original content. Sharing other people's posts will help them, but it won't help you. Creating your own content will always drive more engagement and activity on your own posts.

- Don't use any scheduling tools to push out content to your LinkedIn® newsfeed, you will be penalised for this in less views. LinkedIn® can tell when you have done this, and even worse, so can your connections. Always create the content natively from within LinkedIn®.

- Don't post links to external sites. LinkedIn® makes its money by keeping people within LinkedIn®. When you post and send people away from LinkedIn®, don't expect the post to be seen by a lot of people. You would be better to post the link in the comments.

- Comments on posts need to be more than 4 words in length for LinkedIn® to consider these engagement. So simply having people comment with 'Yes' or an 'A' or 'B' isn't enough for the comments to be considered true engagement. The longer the comments are the better. This is also the case with your replies.

- An engaged view is a minimum of 3 seconds, this applies to all types of posts, not just videos. So for a LinkedIn® members view to count as a view, they need to have remained on the post for at least 3 seconds. I will help you with this when we look at the

5 different styles of LinkedIn® posts in the upcoming section in this chapter.

- As with every aspect of social selling, no selling allowed! You will not get engagement on a post which is purely a sales pitch or an advert. Gary Vaynerchuk says it best. "People want to watch the TV show, not the commercials in between the TV show." They want the story behind your journey and your brand, they love to buy but they don't want to be sold. So avoid any 'call this number' or 'check out my website' or 'contact me' in the text or the video, people know how to reach you through LinkedIn®. Just don't repel them by selling in your content. Attract them!

Engagement is absolutely critical to your success in content visibility on the newsfeed.

Measuring Post Views

Each time you post you can see the amount of views that post receives. There is a small graph at the bottom of each post. If you click that you can see useful information and statistics such as which companies are viewing your post, the job titles that people hold who have viewed the post and which locations they are viewing from.

116

Keep a track of your post views, look at your highest viewed content and learn what worked and what didn't. LinkedIn® regularly changes the algorithm behind post views. Create great content, add value to your connections and engagement will happen. As your network of connections grows, combined with your own confidence in posting, so your post views will increase.

12 Different Content Themes

There are many different types of LinkedIn® posts and various different themes you can get ideas from. Let's start first with the 8 different content themes. I will talk about each in detail. As I do, think about how you could apply that particular post theme in your own business, for your own content.

1. Educational Posts

An educational post is designed to provide value, educate and give help, advice and tips to your target market. You have accumulated so much knowledge and expertise and now it's time to share it. The more you give, the more will come back to you in return. Don't hold back, educate, add value and add even more value. You could share top tips, interview people, create helpful videos and 'how to' clips. Demonstrate your knowledge and share it with the LinkedIn® community. People are more likely to buy from you, the more you give away.

This type of post is easy to create, simply brainstorm all of the topics you would consider yourself to be highly knowledgeable about. Now write down a list under each topic as sub-headings that could be mini-posts about that topic. Every sliver of information you have in your head is a LinkedIn® educational post. You could drip feed help, advice and tips for the next year about what you know, if you just took the time to sit down and list out the knowledge you have.

A great book recommendation for you would be *'They Ask, You Answer'* by Marcus Goldstein. He gives so many strategies on content creation simply by answering the questions that your prospects ask on a day to day basis when you are out selling. An absolutely amazing guide to content creation based on your customers.

Another great tool to use is Answer The Public. You can find this website using the following link: http://AnswerThePublic.com. Simply enter your specialist topic and Answer The Public will give you hundreds of questions that the general public are typing in to search engines. Start by answering them through your posts.

Educational posts are a great way to build your brand, position you as a 'go-to' expert and attract your ideal client towards you.

2. Gratitude Posts

Giving gratitude, saying thank-you, is a great way to help others and thank people in your network for the great support that they have been to you. Use these type of posts on LinkedIn® to give gratitude, tag them in the post so that they are notified.

This is an easy way to bring your brand into their network and to share with people that you give to others by saying thank you. When you give, you gain indirectly, so help others to gain exposure to your network, and you never know what will happen.

Make the post all about the other person, say why you are acknowledging them and suggest that if someone wants a personal introduction to your amazing business contact, to message you directly.

One way you can thank others is by 'Giving Kudos'. Go to the person's LinkedIn® profile that you want to give some kudos to, click in the hidden (…) menu next to the blue message button and choose 'Give Kudos'. There are a number of different ways to thank someone in this way, including being a great mentor, being a team player, being an inspirational leader and so many more. I love this feature if you are a business owner with a team or a manager in a large organisation. What a fantastic way to motivate employees by publicly giving them Kudos to your LinkedIn® network.

3. Documentary Posts

This is my absolute favourite type of post and is one of themes that will drive the most inbound leads to your business, when done well. A documentary post is simply sharing with your network what you are up to.

119

Now I am sure that most days you are going about your business, doing what you do, not even thinking for a second about documenting it, or sharing what you are doing with others. If you don't you are missing a trick!

This is one of the easiest ways to create posts that sell, without selling. This year alone this one theme has generated me in excess of £250,000 in new revenue by simply sharing what I am up to. Every time I speak on stage anywhere in the world, I post about it. Every time I deliver a LinkedIn® Masterclass I post about it. Every time I deliver a workshop to help delegates get their LinkedIn® profile sorted, I post about it. Every time I am creating content, I post about it. Every time I secure a win for a client, I post about it. You get the idea...

Documenting what you are doing is social proof that you are out there doing what you do and getting results for your clients. The best way to think about this theme is to look back over your calendar for the last 7-14 days.

- Where have you been?

- What events, conferences or seminars have you attended?

- Who have you met with?

- What results have you had achieved for your clients?

- What have you done personally?

- What have you done professionally?

- What have you learnt?

- What have you read?

All of these can be turned into LinkedIn® posts that simply document what you have been up to. When you master these documentary style posts you will really be selling without selling. All it takes is for someone in your target market to see the post and inbox you saying 'I've been following your posts on LinkedIn®' and for them to identify with what you have been doing to help others just like them.

You never know who is seeing your posts, you never know who in your extended network is going to see your posts. I recently won a new Corporate Client, a multi-billion ££ turnover company, who came to me because I was regularly sharing documentary style posts. One of my 1st degree connections was commenting on and liking my posts, and a Commercial Director, who I was not connected to in any way, reached out to me because one of their Sales Managers had been seeing me pop up in his newsfeed regularly delivering LinkedIn® Masterclasses and in-house training. When asked to recommend a Social Selling strategist and LinkedIn® expert he named me and I won the business.

4. Controversial Posts

These are not going to be for everyone, but they drive massive engagement very quickly.

This is where you post about a controversial topic and in doing so divide opinion. People love to have a rant on LinkedIn®. Be sensible here, so avoid anything non-PC, topics such as politics and religion etc. You still need to protect your personal brand and remember that you are highly visible in posts like this. After all *"The way you do anything, is the way you do everything"*.

Let's say for example that I wanted to do a post about LinkedIn® vs. Facebook. I could have a very strong argument for LinkedIn® yet others in my network may feel very strongly about Facebook. I could write a post that invited discussion underneath and before long the comments would be getting momentum and the post would potentially go viral on LinkedIn®.

I could start a post with 'LinkedIn®, don't bother…" now as a LinkedIn® expert people may be shocked at me starting a post with these words, and may jump on the post to defend. But in the long form text of the post or video, I could go on to explain that there is no point in bothering with LinkedIn® unless you understand your target market and understand the key principles of social selling, outlined in the first section of this book.

Have some fun with this theme!

5. Wins and Success Posts

Earlier this year, I was delivering a Masterclass and in the room there was an expert in Oil & Gas recruitment, Mark. He had never posted on LinkedIn® before and when we started talking about this theme, he could not believe that anyone would be remotely interested in what he was up to, his successes in business or how it could create him inbound leads. My Masterclasses are highly practical, so after I had taught the class the theory on content creation, we as a group all posted a piece of content on LinkedIn® together. He chose to create a post highlighting some success he had been having.

He shared in his first ever LinkedIn® post how he had successfully placed 3 senior level candidates in the Middle East in the Oil and Gas industry in challenging roles that the client had been struggling to fill, and how the clients were over the moon and it had led to him having his best quarter ever. Now due to the confidential nature of his work, he could not mention the name of the companies or the candidates he had placed. But nevertheless, it was a great post designed to tap into a prospects pain points, and demonstrate his expertise in his niche.

The Masterclass delegates jumped on his post to help it generate some engagement quickly, they all do that for each other in the classroom. Within 2 hours of the post going live, Mark had received an inbound lead from an old contact of his who he had worked with 7 years prior, he had not realised that Mark had set up his own business and he resonated with the post, because he had been struggling to fill some challenging roles himself in the oil and gas sector. He walked out of the Masterclass with a meeting and 3 new vacancies to work on. He couldn't believe it!

So the lesson here is: share your wins and successes. The LinkedIn® ecosystem is a supportive place where people will follow your journey and celebrate your success. Don't underestimate the power of this theme. Inbound leads will come from these types of posts, your connections will message you and you will turn your contacts into contracts.

6. Social Proof & Reviews

Have you ever received a gift from a client after doing a great job? What about a text message, email or phone call? What about a hand-written thank you card? Each time you do, it's social proof that you are great at what you do and also it's an amazing LinkedIn® post. We talked about the power of personal recommendations on LinkedIn® earlier, those can also be turned into posts.

Use the opportunity to tag the person who thanked you for the great work (with their permission of course). Thank them for the lovely gift, card, text, message etc. and put up a picture of whatever you received. When you have happy customers and others see that you will attract more people towards you.

I regularly receive cards, champagne, flowers, gifts and cards in my office (which is amazing!) from clients who have loved their time on a Masterclass, or people that have generated massive results from LinkedIn® as a result of my knowledge. I post about these and share this with my LinkedIn® connections.

Testimonials, reviews, cards, gifts, whatever format they arrive in you can turn this social proof into great LinkedIn® posts. If you received a review on Facebook, or on Google my business or Amazon, then take a screenshot and post it!

When you demonstrate consistently that your clients appreciate you, then you will build your personal brand and increase the trust with potential clients that you are great at what you do.

7. News Updates

This is an easy theme. It's simple. What news do you have about your career, your business, your company, your products, your services, your team? The list goes on. What news can you share that continues to demonstrate that you are busy, growing, doing great things and making things better for your customers.

- If you have taken on a new team member, announce it to your LinkedIn® network

- If you have formed a strategic partnership or alliance, announce it

- If you have won an award, share it with your LinkedIn® network

- If you are attending a conference or trade show, announce it to your network

- If you just got a promotion or moved jobs, share it

All of this, as usual, needs to be done in a way that is selling without selling. You will find that people will react to a post like this with comments and the 'Celebrate' reaction on LinkedIn® if you aren't using it as a sales pitch.

8. Ask a Question

This last theme could be used across all of the previous seven themes. Asking a question on a LinkedIn® post, will drive answers in the comments, which in turn equals engagement.

I was recently training in-house with a corporate sales and marketing team. The UK marketing director was in the training and was excited about heading to London to attend an awards ceremony. He created a post about it, which built the credibility of the brand and shared what he was up to. In itself, on its own, it would not have driven a lot of engagement, reactions yes, but not comments. So I suggested he ask a question.

The question we added to the post was "What is the best award you have ever won?". Within minutes the post had started to drive a lot of responses and by the time he left that afternoon there were more than 20 comments on the post, with people sharing their best award.

When you ask a question or ask for feedback, your LinkedIn® network will respond. Let's say you are re-branding. You may have a choice of a few different logos or colours to choose from, why not ask your LinkedIn® network to help you decide. Responses will come in the form of comments and you will drive engagement on your post.

Before we move on to look at the different styles of posts, and how to actually create a post on LinkedIn®, choose a theme from the 8 themes I have just covered and decide which one you like the most.

9. Inspirational

LinkedIn® posts that inspire your network are a great idea, you don't have to be some thought leader or well known in business to be inspirational. People love to be inspired and posts that share an inspirational message can work really well.

I am not talking about quotes and memes, like you see on Facebook, I am talking about well thought out, long form text posts designed to share a message or videos that inspire.

Maybe you or someone close to you has been through adversity, either now or in the past. It's part of your make up. Being vulnerable and sharing your story can be one of the best ways to connect with your audience.

You just don't know who needs to hear your message. Someone who has been where you have, or is going through it right now, needs to be inspired by you.

10.   Mindset & Motivational

Mental toughness is a hot topic at the moment. I firmly believe that mindset is everything when it comes to winning in life and business. Posts that focus on the power of mindset, visualisation, motivation and belief are always great themes.

You may choose to share motivation from others, or on occasion you may have a post that focuses on how you faced a challenge and how mindset and beliefs helped you to overcome it.

11.   Learnings Along the Way

Your journey in your career or your business is going to teach you a great deal. Posts that share what you did, and what you learnt as a result, are great themes for LinkedIn® posts.

It could be about a seminar or event you attended, a book you read, a podcast the you learnt from, an interview you watch, an audible book that you listened to. Maybe you tried something new in your business and it worked or you tried something new and it didn't.

Either way, you are learning all of the time and by sharing what you did and what you learnt from your experience you will be adding massive value to your network.

12. Personal Posts

I often get asked about whether you should post about your personal life on LinkedIn®. My view is that there is always a business spin on a personal post. For example, I posted from my holiday in Italy, having stood in the Colosseum in Rome, I created a piece of content about how Rome wasn't built in a day, how important it is to be patient in business and not always seek instant gratification. I will often post about my kids, but linked to their involvement in our business, so Maya has a baking business which she started at age 10 and she provides cakes and treats for all of our delegates who attend Masterclasses. I post about my passion for kids enterprise and young entrepreneurship. I post about my role as a Business Ambassador in schools, I post about personal goal setting. I see others post about sporting achievements in their personal life, but linking these back into a business context. So bring your personal life into the LinkedIn® newsfeed to add another angle to you, to increase connection in other ways to your network and add value at the same time

Use the space below to write down your ideas for 3 different LinkedIn® posts:

IDEA 1:

_____

_____

_____

IDEA 2:

_____

_____

_____

IDEA 3:

_____

_____

_____

Now that you have your 12 different themes, let's look at 4 different styles of posts you can create using images, video, documents and text.

4 Different Styles of LinkedIn® Posts

This next section will help you with the actual style of post; we have looked at the themes, what you are going to post about.

Now I am going to give you 5 different styles of post that you can currently use on LinkedIn® to create your content.

1. Text Posts - Short Form vs. Long Form

When you post on LinkedIn®, only the first three lines of text can be seen, after that a button called *'See More…'* shows up.

A short post will be no longer than three lines. It's a simple piece of text. A long form post makes the *'See More…'* button appear. The more people who click on *'See More…'* the more views and the more momentum you will create on your post. Make the first three lines count, and use curiosity to get them to click on *'See More…'*.

LinkedIn® absolutely <u>LOVES</u> long posts, so keep your short form text posts to a minimum. If you don't have much time use this style of post, but don't expect it to gain as much visibility as when you use lots of text.

The same applies when you post photos and videos, you will gain more visibility and views the longer the text that accompanies it. Remember, LinkedIn® likes to keep the members in LinkedIn®, and the longer your posts are the longer it takes to read them. Which is why you will always get more views, the longer the text on any type of post.

2. Image / Photograph Posts

It is important that your content caters for all different learning styles. Always remember that 70% of LinkedIn® members will prefer visual communication so posts including photographs and images should be a part of your content strategy.

Images can be those you have taken yourself on your smartphone, or you can use royalty free images. There are some fantastic websites you can use to find great photographs for your posts.

These include: pixabay.com, pexels.com and unsplash.com. It is important not to use images you find on Google as you could get into issues with copyright. When you use sites that are community led with royalty-free photos, you can search for keywords that represent what you are posting about.

You can post multiple images or a single image on LinkedIn®. The combination that works best is odd numbers, so 1 image, 3 images or 5 images. They just seem to show up better on the mobile newsfeed and desktop versions of LinkedIn® in that combination.

When you add multiple images you are making a collage effect. You can tag people into your photographs and add stickers to them when you post. I usually try to post 2 or 3 image posts per week. Often I will use photos with documentary theme posts and success/wins themed posts, these seem to work the best with photographs.

3. Document Posts

The most recent type of post to be added to LinkedIn® is a document post. This is where you can upload a file such as a PDF, Word Document, or Slide Show to educate your network on a specific topic. Ideas for these types of posts include case studies, white papers, tip sheets, presentation slides.

The last two document posts I have created have exceeded 14,000 views in both cases with a lot less engagement and reactions than my normal posts.

John Espirian is one of the best people to follow on LinkedIn®, he delivers great document posts that are super helpful for all aspects of LinkedIn® content as well as copywriting, technical tips for all sorts of social media and content hacks.

You can connect with John Espirian at https://www.linkedin.com/in/johnespirian/. Mention that you learnt about him in this book when you connect. John has found recently that his document posts get shared more than any other type of content he produces. It's early days, but he is getting great results from document style posts.

4. Video Posts

Take a moment to pick up your mobile phone. Go to the LinkedIn® app and scroll down the newsfeed to 30-60 seconds. Count how many videos you can see.

You will probably get into double figures. It is clear that video posts are by far the most engaging and popular on LinkedIn®. So what this tells us is that video HAS to be a part of your content marketing.

Less than 4% of LinkedIn® members are posting video content, so the great thing here is that you can gain competitive edge and build your personal brand through video whilst it is still relatively under utilised.

As I mentioned earlier in this chapter, 85% of video content on social media is viewed without sound, therefore it is important that you include captions on your videos. A great service you can use for this is rev.com. Send your movies off to Rev and within hours you will have an SRT file back from them with the transcript of the video. You will pay $1.00 per minute of video on rev.com and they are 99.8% accurate.

Another service you may want to consider is QUICC (http://www.quicc.io/welcome?fpr=samrathling). At the time of writing this is still in beta test mode but is an alternative solution for captions. I have recently become an Ambassador for QUICC and I am loving what the QUICC team are doing to make video content simple.

When you upload the movie file on LinkedIn®, you can edit the video and simply add the SRT file. Or you can use video editing software such as kapwing.com or iMovie to edit your videos and add in the subtitles.

There are also apps available to help you caption your videos. I love 'Clip-O-Matic' which puts captions on to your videos in real time. It's a paid for app, for £4.99 in the App Store. I like to use this for recording personalised messages to people and then sending video messages, which we spoke about in the previous chapter.

LinkedIn® LIVE!

At the time of writing this book, LinkedIn® Live! Video is being tested in beta mode with a number of content creators globally. It will be rolled out eventually to all LinkedIn® members, although they first need to make it robust and then it will take months to roll out such a major new feature.

I plan to use it when I get access to it, and I highly recommend that you start using it as soon as you gain access to LinkedIn® Live! I cannot wait for it to arrive properly to the wider LinkedIn® community.

Using #hashtags

Hashtags are relatively new to LinkedIn®. When you post your content from the homepage, simply add hashtags using the # symbol. Adding hashtags to your LinkedIn® updates and articles gives them a higher chance of being discovered by LinkedIn® members, who follow or search for the hashtag you've used. Hashtags can be placed after copy, or embedded within copy on your posts so long as it makes sense to do so.

When you post a great piece of content, it can be picked up by the LinkedIn® Algorithm and your post can start trending with that hashtag, which will increase your visibility. People who you may not even be connected with on LinkedIn® will see the post because they follow that hashtag. I use #socialselling on my posts as one of my main hashtags. I was recently invited to appear on a podcast by an expert in Australia after he found me because I was using #socialselling on my posts. He follows this hashtag because it interests him, we were not connected at all, he wasn't even in my 2nd or 3rd degree network, but he came across me because of the hashtag I was using.

To see how many people are following a LinkedIn® hashtag, enter the hashtag ideas you have for your personal and/or company brand in the main LinkedIn® search bar.

The results will show how many members are following that specific hashtag.

Here are some of the most popular hashtags on LinkedIn®.

General

#Mindfulness #Creativity #Leadership #Innovation #Management #Motivation #Tips #Productivity #Careers #GettingThingsDone #MentalHealth #Inspiration

Social Media & Marketing

#Branding #KnowYourSocial #SocialNetworking #SocialMedia #SocialMediaMarketing #SocialMediaAdvertising #DigitalMarketing #ContentMarketing #OnlineAdvertising #Marketing #Sales

Small Business & Entrepreneurship

#Business #BusinessIntelligence #SmallBusiness #Entrepreneur #Entrepreneurship #SocialEntrpreneurship

Like hashtags elsewhere, LinkedIn® hashtags can only include letters, numbers and emoji.

Any spaces or symbols used will break the link. That means you cannot use apostrophes, commas, exclamation points, or hyphens. Here are some key punctuation do's and don'ts when it comes to hashtags:

- DON'T add spaces. Multiple word hashtags should be grouped together. For example: #JustDoIt not #Just Do It.

- DO capitalise multi-word hashtags. Titlecasing will vastly improve readability and will prevent hashtags from being read incorrectly

- DON'T use symbols or punctuation marks. English teachers will cringe over turning I'm into Im or you're into youre, but hashtags operate under their own rules

- DO include punctuation around your hashtag. If your hashtag is in a sentence and should be followed by a comma, end mark, or other form of punctuation, including one will not affect the tag

- DO check your spelling. Hashtags can often be overlooked in proofreads, but a misspelled hashtag is never a good thing

There are no limits to the number of hashtags you can use in a post on LinkedIn®. That said, I recommend that you limit each post to a maximum of 3-5 hashtags. Using too many hashtags on LinkedIn® could also result in the LinkedIn® algorithm marking your post as spam.

LinkedIn® will automatically suggested relevant hashtags when you begin to write a post. If they seem like a good fit, include them. But don't add them just for the sake of it.

Be deliberate in your hashtag use.

Be aware that there is a niche community online for every industry and subject, and they often use specific hashtags. Using the right niche hashtag will connect you to an online community that's passionate about your industry. Look for industry-specific LinkedIn® hashtags at https://www.linkedin.com/feed/follow-hashtags/. Make sure to also check Instagram, Twitter, Reddit or other online forums for inspiration on hashtags.

Start following hashtags relevant to your brand. Posts with the hashtags you decide to follow will show up in your LinkedIn® feed. A list of the hashtags you already follow on LinkedIn® can be found from the homepage in the left sidebar under *'Your communities'*.

You can start following existing LinkedIn® hashtags in a few ways, but the easiest way is to add them from https://www.linkedin.com/feed/follow-hashtags/.

Click each hashtag to get a glimpse of how others are using them. Look to see if members of LinkedIn® are using additional hashtags that you could be following and using, too.

If you are reading this book representing a large brand, brands can also use LinkedIn® Elevate (https://www.linkedin.com/elevate/) to create a company hashtag (https://www.linkedin.com/help/linkedin/answer/90434). The company hashtag can be automatically appended to employee posts, which helps to increase the visibility of your company and tag company-related content. For further inspiration, click Discover more (https://www.linkedin.com/feed/follow/?filterType=channel&focused=true) at the bottom of your hashtag list.

Tagging People in Posts

I have mentioned tagging people a number of times in this chapter, always make sure your tags are relevant. Don't simply tag people because they have a lot of connections (it really annoys me when people do that!).

Always make sure its permission based, or they were an active part of your status update, ie. that you were with them at an event, you are thanking them personally or they are in a picture or video you are posting.

Simply use the @ symbol and start typing their name in a post with a space in-between their first and last name, the people with that name will show up in a drop-down list. Simply select them and they will be tagged. Their name will show up bold in either blue or black depending on which device you are using.

They will be notified that you have tagged them in their notifications, which will encourage them to engage with the post and will ensure that the post is seen by their network as well as yours.

5 Actionable Insights:

1. Post daily on LinkedIn®, and engage with everyone who comments.

2. Choose different themes for your posts to mix up your content marketing.

3. Post different types of posts to mix up the appeal to different learning styles.

4. Use hashtags and tags in every post to get your content found by a wider audience.

5. Always direct your content at your exact target market, but never, ever sell.

CHAPTER 8
Positioning your Expertise

When you are considered as 'go-to' person in your industry you will ATTRACT clients towards you like a magnet. You will never have to go looking for business as it will come to you. You will be referred, others will be talking about you and your personal brand will be so strong that you become oversubscribed with a waiting list of people wanting to work with you.

I learnt about this concept back in 2011 when I was just starting out life as a speaker. Back then when I was new to the expert world, I would be asked to speak about business networking, referral marketing, online networking (including LinkedIn®) and building relationships. My topics were quite broad and there were quite a few other speakers out there covering the same kind of topics.

Then I attended an event with my business coach at the time, where I saw Daniel Priestly speaking about his new book KPI: Key Person of Influence. He shared 5 things that were important when building a personal brand. One of them, being the importance of picking a niche. I now know that you can never be too niche! The more niche you are the easier it is to refer you, attract the right kind of clients and build a business where people value what you do, value your expertise and you can charge more for your products and services when you are seen as the 'go-to' version of you in your industry and/or geography.

After learning this, I went from being a generalist who spoke broadly about networking to a specialist in LinkedIn®. I then wrote the first version of this book in 2013 and started to get booked to speak only about LinkedIn®, so gradually I have transitioned from being a specialist in a niche to now becoming an expert authority on this topic. My focus is now on becoming the #1 name associated with social selling through LinkedIn®, globally. It's taken me years to develop my personal brand, my name, my expert positioning. Now I am here, I am able to charge more, generate 400+ inbound leads a month, attract my ideal client towards me and pick and choose which events I speak at.

There are 4 levels of expert positioning and I will talk through each one. As I do, think about where you currently sit and look at how you can apply this knowledge to your personal brand.

Level 1: Generalists

Many people who do what you do are generalists, along with about 85% of the market, these people cut prices to compete, and they are fighting to win new clients claiming to be everything to everyone.

These people earn the least amount of money, are typically sub £100k in annual turnover and are always struggling financially because they have no defined niche or expertise. This may be you, or not, either way the quicker you move out of the generalist space the better.

You can find generalists in every sector. Think about who you compete with and also analyse your own business; are you one of thousands of generalists? If so, you will find it much harder to stand out on LinkedIn®.

A great additional resource to help you understand this would be *'Blue Ocean Strategy'* by Renée Mauborgne and W. Chan Kim. It's all about how to make your competition irrelevant and find marketing opportunities that set you apart from the rest.

Level 2: Specialists

The next level up is 'Specialists', these are people who have chosen to specialise in a particular area and consists of about 13% of the market. Here are some examples:

- A Website Designer who specialises only in helping Insurance Brokers
- A Financial Advisor specialising in families with children who have special needs
- A Business Coach who specialises in helping Social Enterprises & Non-Profits

- A Chiropractor who specialises in helping children with ADHD
- A Printer who specialises only in printing exercise books and training manuals
- A Graphic Designer who specialises only in Magazine Design

Think about this, if you had a problem with your back and you were in a lot of pain, you could go to your GP, a generalist who looks after the whole body. Or you could go to a specialist who only looks after that specific type of pain, and could instantly fix your problem. Most of you would choose the specialist.

Would you expect to pay more or less to see a specialist? More! You get the idea, so being a specialist allows you to charge more and attract more of the right type of client.

Now apply this to your LinkedIn® activity. Your LinkedIn® profile can demonstrate your speciality, speaking directly to your niche target market. Your LinkedIn® content can speak about your speciality and demonstrate your expertise. Then you can write articles that reflect your credibility in working specifically with that type of client. Suddenly you are going to have significant credibility against your competition, and gain significant market share in your space.

Ask yourself these questions to help identify your specialisation:

1. What could you do to specialise more?
2. Where does your passion lie? Who do you LOVE helping?
3. What type of clients would you really like to have more of, if you could choose?
4. What have you done in your career that could enhance that specialisation?
5. Look at your last 20 clients, what common theme is there?

Level 3: Authority Expert

When you become an Authority Expert on a particular subject then you start to really ramp up your visibility and credibility. There is only a very small percentage (2%) of people in your field who elevate themselves to this level.

There is no co-incidence that the word 'Authority' has the word 'Author' in it! If you want to become an authority or be seen as an expert in your field, then the best activity you could work on is writing a book or producing a podcast, or creating amazing amounts of content that position you as someone who knows what they are talking about.

You will see that your credibility skyrockets, you will attract people to your profile on LinkedIn® and other social media sites, and you will be booked more for both consultancy work and speaking opportunities if you are considered an Expert Authority in your chosen line of work.

This takes years and years of application, but if you are prepared to work hard you can go from being a specialist to absolutely dominating your space. I set out in 2011 to achieve this with my personal brand and only now in 2019 am I really reaping the benefits of this.

I am officially the most expensive LinkedIn® Trainer in the UK. I am more than 10 times more expensive than most other LinkedIn® and Social Selling experts who are in this bracket, and I am 50 times more expensive than most people who are in the generalist category of 'Social Media' with no expertise or specialisation in any platform. I am not for everyone, but there are companies out there who are prepared to pay for the most expensive version of you.

Years ago, when no-one knew who I was, I would struggle to find new clients, I would have to work really hard to get new business in, I would speak for free all the time and I was competing on price when I pitched for new business, I was running around the UK like a lunatic chasing business. It was REALLY difficult, I had to be mentally strong and focus on building up my personal brand.

Today, I am fortunate to be able to pick and choose who I work with, new clients come to me daily in all 3 sets of my target market and I now have the expert positioning with my personal brand that I set my sights on back in 2011.

Do I have competition? Yes, absolutely. But now I have the track record, the social proof and the results for clients to back up my credibility in my space. When a Corporate Client pays me my full day rate, I know how quickly they are going to get their return and can evidence that in the results I achieve for my clients.

So how can you apply this?

1. Set a goal for your ideal pricing of your products and services and write them down. Even if you think that no-one would pay that for what you do, think BIG! What are you truly worth?

2. Now put a zero on the end of it. And gulp! When you position yourself as the 'go-to' expert in your field you can start to charge more for what you do and truly start charging your worth. The biggest barrier to this will be the 6 inches between your ears and the little voice in your head that's telling you already that you cannot charge that or be paid that amount. Your money mindset is going to be the biggest blockage to you being paid what you should be for what you do

3. Test this out. Next time you tell someone how much your services are going to cost, double your usual price. When they say 'yes', send me a message, celebrate and make

that your new price. When you get comfortable with this, do it again

I remember back in 2016 going to work with a client in Nottingham, I spent the day with him and his team and shared some social selling strategies and showed them how to prospect effectively. He asked for my price, and then negotiated me down, so I discounted my day rate to win the business. One month later he informed me that he had closed £63,000 in new business. Three months later he texted me to let me know that they had landed a contract with an initial value of £750,000.

So that was £813,000 in new business just 90 days after me training him and his team. I had charged just £750 for the day. Today I charge in excess of £20,000 per day for in-house training and I don't blink an eye when I tell a Corporate Client how much it will cost to work with me. That's the power of becoming an Expert Authority.

Number One Celebrity

When I use the word celebrity, it does not mean Hollywood film star or pop sensation, it means that you are the #1 'go-to' person globally for what you do.

Let's look at some examples:

The #1 in Life Coaching and NLP Transformations and Breakthroughs is Tony Robbins.

The #1 in Networking is Dr. Ivan Misner, founder of BNI (Business Network International)

The #1 in Presenting Talk Shows & Interviewing would be Oprah (35,000 interviews!)

The #1 in Social Media Trends & Social Media Strategy would be Gary Vaynerchuk

The #1 in Property Investment would be Grant Cardone with a $1.2bn property portfolio

You get the idea. Most of these people have written multiple best-selling books and are world famous. It is unlikely you will have heard of all of them, but most likely you have heard of at least one of them.

So how does this all relate to LinkedIn®? The next set of tips are all going to focus on how you can start to position yourself on LinkedIn® as someone who knows what they are talking about in your chosen field of expertise.

Write Articles on LinkedIn® That Reflect Your Expertise

In Chapter 7 we covered creating amazing content leveraging the LinkedIn® newsfeed. When it comes to positioning yourself as an expert on a particular topic, LinkedIn® articles can be a great way to build up your credibility and demonstrate that you know your subject matter.

Articles will never receive as much attention or views as posts in the newsfeed, but that's not why you should write them. Articles are evergreen, meaning that stay on LinkedIn® forever, and can be accessed directly from your LinkedIn® profile. When someone reads an article you have written, at the bottom LinkedIn® shares more articles from the same Author. They are a great way to drive people back to your website, to your landing pages, sales funnels and to drive calls to action to encourage someone to engage with you at the next level.

I recommend posting an article once per month as a minimum, these are like blogs, although within the LinkedIn® environment. If you are already blogging, you can repurpose your blogs as LinkedIn® articles. In order to avoid affecting your SEO and Google rankings take blogs that are more than 3 months old, and if you do publish a new blog be sure to make some changes to the headline and body if using it on LinkedIn®.

An article needs to be packed FULL of value. Sharing your best tips, advice and knowledge to demonstrate that you really know what you are talking about. Each article should be somewhere between 1000 and 3000 words, not just a quick couple of paragraphs. Really take the time to deliver value and insights that others will want to engage with, create discussions about and share.

151

The great thing about an article is that you can also use videos, images, quotes and insert links to back up your text within the article. So if you have a YouTube channel you can embed your YouTube video about the same subject and encourage people to subscribe, even though they originally found you through a LinkedIn® article. Unlike with content in the LinkedIn® newsfeed, you are not penalised for adding links to external sites within an article. So you can drive traffic back to your website or other social media channels.

Always use an attention grabbing headline. The top of your article needs a fantastic image as this will draw people towards your content. Remember you can use images from pixabay.com, pexels.com and unsplash.com to find suitable, high impact images that represent your article well. Then write in a way that breaks down your topic into simple steps and is easy to read. Include images, videos and quotes within the text, to keep it interesting.

I always recommend using an 'About the Author' section at the bottom of every article so that you have a standard way of signing off your articles, and include links to your other social media sites, and how to contact you. This makes it easy for someone who likes what you are sharing to get in touch with you.

Finally include a call to action at the end of the article. Encourage the readers to comment below, that will drive engagement on your article and as with content, as you read in Chapter 7, the more engagement the article receives the more likely it will be shared and given visibility by LinkedIn®.

Unlike posts that you create in the LinkedIn® newsfeed, you can save Articles and publish them later. You can share a draft with a colleague before it goes live. When you publish the article, it goes into the normal newsfeed as an Article, so ensure you include hashtags and some context to the article when you first post it so that your network know what it is about.

Always remember to keep your exact target market top of mind when you are writing articles. The article needs to speak to them, address their pain points and be helpful to them. You will never appeal to every single person, that doesn't matter. Write with your prospects in mind. Your most recent article appears on your LinkedIn® profile directly underneath your 'About' section. It adds credibility to your profile when potential clients can see that you are also creating great content that is relevant to them.

Profile Yourself as a Speaker on LinkedIn®

Even if you are new to public speaking, you can use your LinkedIn® profile to position yourself as a Speaker on your subject. Even if you have only done a few local events, and even if they were not paid you can really start to use your LinkedIn® presence to get invited to speak at more events. You can offer yourself as a speaker through organisations, networks, professional bodies and more. Your LinkedIn® profile could get you booked for many speaking engagements especially if you choose a niche that few people occupy.

If you are going to dominate in your chosen field of expertise then you should learn the skills you need to present in front of an audience, you can highlight your speaking topics and experience on your LinkedIn® profile.

This won't be for everyone, but if you work LinkedIn® well and focus on this aspect of your niche then you will find that you get booked more and more, and you can start charging more for what you do.

I regularly get booked to speak at conferences and events as an expert on LinkedIn® and Social Selling.

When I first started out building my personal brand this was one of the best ways to build my profile and improve my positioning. Each time I am on a stage I get video footage and photography taken to boost social proof that I am out there regularly speaking on my topic and it leads to inbound leads.

When on stage I use the 'Find Nearby' feature on the LinkedIn®, which is on the mobile app, to connect the room with each other and grow my connections with raving fans who have heard me on stage. I also use the LinkedIn® QR code on my slides to ensure that I can connect with everyone in the audience.

You will find this feature in the search bar on the mobile app, it's a small icon within the search bar and takes you to a screen where you can either scan or see your own code. Here is mine as an example.

Why not try it now? Get your mobile phone, go to the LinkedIn® mobile app and click on the small icon in the search bar. Now scan my QR code on this page. It will work on a hard copy of this book or an electronic version depending on what format you are reading in.

When you are in this part of LinkedIn® you have the option to save your code to your photos. Now you can include this on your slides when you present to an audience and instruct them all to go to their search bar in LinkedIn® and scan your code to add you as a connection.

Just say "I would love to speak to each of you 1:1 but given the size of this audience I'm not going to get to you all. So If you

155

have any questions about what I've shared and want to continue to learn from me, then add me on LinkedIn® using this QR code."

NOTE: If speaking is going to become part of your strategy for building your professional brand and positioning you as a 'go-to' expert, then I highly recommend that you go along to your local PSA regional meeting. This is the Professional Speaking Association, where you can learn how to speak more and speak better. I belong to the East Midlands region and you can learn more at this website: http://thepsa.co.uk.

Track your Profile Views & Search Results Statistics

Your profile views can be found on your 'Dashboard' in your LinkedIn® profile. It looks like this:

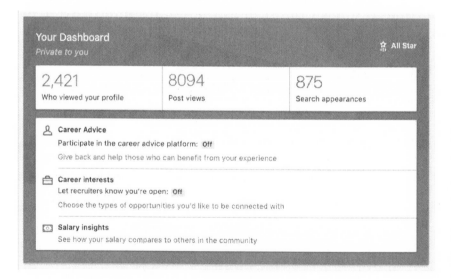

These statistics are important for tracking your visibility and credibility. The total number of people who have viewed your profile is a 90 day statistic. The Search appearances is a 7 days statistic. The more you build your personal brand and expertise, the more you will see these numbers increase.

Go have a look at your own numbers now and record them here.

Who's Viewed Your Profile: _____

Date: _____

Search Appearances: _____

Date: _____

I refer to these numbers as your 'Visibility Factor'. The more times people are visiting your profile and you are appearing in search results, the more your personal brand is developing. Once you start applying everything in this book, your profile views will increase and so will your search appearances all the time and you are attracting people to your profile through all of the techniques we have shared here.

The great news is that whatever your number is today, it is going to go up considerably by just taking a few small simple steps to increase your visibility. Add to this great content, recommendations and a fantastic profile and you will be increasing both your visibility and credibility. The one other

157

number to focus on is the number of Followers you have. When you have more followers than you do connections, that's when you start to have influence. Influence is key in building your expertise and positioning in your niche.

5 Quick Tips:

1. Look at where you are now and set a goal for where you want to be in your positioning

2. Choose your niche, could you niche even more within that niche?

3. Write Articles and publish them on LinkedIn®, decide on your first 3 topics

4. Download your LinkedIn® QR code and start using it

5. Check your Visibility Stats and log them today so you can track your performance

CHAPTER 9
Pages: Build your Company Brand

Having a Company Page on LinkedIn® is essential. It gives you and your company the opportunity to take part in conversations important to your brand, engage with and grow your audience, and leverage your current employees to spread your brand message.

Most of what I have focussed on so far in this book has been about building your personal brand, now it's time to turn our attention to your Company Brand.

It is important to be aware that your LinkedIn® Company Page will never replace your LinkedIn® personal profile in its importance and ability to generate new leads, but there are 5 key reasons for having a LinkedIn® Company Page:

1. Recruiting & Attracting Great Talent to your Organisation

2. Spreading your Company message through your Employees

3. Raising brand awareness for your Company Brand, Products & Services

4. Promoting CSR (Corporate Social Responsibility) efforts

5. It's an additional way for you and your Company to be found

If you are reading this book and you work for an organisation that employs 10-200 people, you are growing, recruiting and scaling or you already work for an enterprise level company with more than 200 employees, then pay attention to this Chapter. You will already have a company page, someone will have previously set one up' How active it is and the extent to which it is driving engagement, is going to be largely down to your marketing department.

If you are reading this and you are currently a micro or start up business, my advice would be to focus on building your personal brand, through your LinkedIn® personal profile with a limited focus on your Company Page. You should definitely build a Company Page (using the instructions I am going to give you in this chapter), so that you have a presence. But, what I am saying is, don't focus energy and time on content and followers until you are more established.

Be aware that your company page is linked from your personal profile. Once you have created your company page the logo of your Company, will appear next to your work experience and your employees will be able to link themselves to your business.

Whether you are a micro-business or larger company, not having a company page will not affect your credibility.

LinkedIn® Pages Rebranded

In November 2018, LinkedIn® relaunched 'Company Pages' as 'LinkedIn® Pages', adding new features that you may not be aware of. If you log into LinkedIn® today, you'll notice some obvious differences. Understanding these new LinkedIn® updates will help you take advantage of all that LinkedIn® Pages has to offer. Here's what you need to know about LinkedIn® Pages.

Whatever you specialise in, you want your company to be part of the conversation. More than half of LinkedIn®'s traffic comes from their mobile app, but a number of the benefits that individual users enjoy in the mobile app have not been extended to LinkedIn® Page admins. LinkedIn®'s mobile app does allow you to post, update, and respond to comments from anywhere, making it easier to manage the conversations in which your company is taking part.

Ensure that you have someone dedicated to managing the LinkedIn® company page, or a team of people in a larger organisation. You can have a number of page administrators, allowing multiple people from your sales or, in most cases, marketing division to act as the company on LinkedIn®. LinkedIn® Pages enables you to participate in conversations, and respond to comments as the company page.

161

Content on LinkedIn® Pages

I have already covered a great deal about content in the previous Chapter 7, mostly around what to post to build your personal brand. The additional types of content to add on LinkedIn® pages would be:

- Interviews with Leadership Team Members
- Interviews with staff about what it is like to work for your Company
- Roles you have open and are recruiting for
- Case Studies and White Papers
- Press Releases and Company Updates
- Brand Stories
- Customer Success Stories
- Partner & Channel related news
- Culture, Values, Mission focus
- Behind the Scenes Action
- New Hires, Promotions, Career Moves
- The Story of Your Brand

Once you start creating and sharing content that interests the Followers of your page (your audience), you need to determine whether or not your content strategy is successful. LinkedIn® Pages now give administrators stronger visual analytics that can be used to further understand your success on the platform.

You can filter your dashboard by any time frame to determine how you are performing over time, and adjust your strategy accordingly. All admins will receive a monthly summary email, providing them with the demographics of people visiting the site and which content they are interacting with.

You can share the exact same types of posts from LinkedIn® Pages that I covered earlier including text, links, photographs, video and documents. The same rules apply to LinkedIn® pages as personal posts.

Know & Grow your Followers

Your success as a Company brand is tied to your ability to understand your audience, people can 'follow' your LinkedIn® page. The more keyed into the unique challenges, pain points and needs of your audience or followers, the stronger your content will be, and the more it will resonate with your audience. This goes back to what I covered earlier in the section on your personal brand.

To help you understand exactly what content is resonating with your audience, LinkedIn® Pages offers "Content Suggestions." With content suggestions, simply select your audience, and you'll be presented with a list of topics and articles they are interested in. Create original content based around these topics, or share articles your audience is already interested. This update makes it easier than ever to stay active on LinkedIn®, which will drive traffic to your page and increase your follower count.

163

Once you start creating and sharing content that interests your audience, you need to determine whether or not your content strategy is successful. LinkedIn® Pages now give administrators stronger visual analytics that can be used to further understand your success as a brand.

You can filter your dashboard by any time frame to determine how you are performing and adjust your strategy accordingly.

Engage & Empower your Staff

Engagement is just as critical on a company post as it is on a post from your personal profile. The advantage you have as a larger enterprise is that all of your employees can follow your Company LinkedIn® Page and interact, react, and share with their own networks. Imagine having a sales team of 100+ trained on the power of social selling, all sharing updates from your LinkedIn® page. The reach into all of their extended networks is massive. Employees generally have ten times the reach of a company on LinkedIn®, making them a great resource for expanding your brand's reach.

Not enough attention is given to how you can leverage your current employees to grow your brand. With the updates to LinkedIn® Pages, admins of your Company page will now receive a notification every time your company is tagged in a post. These posts can easily be shared to your LinkedIn® Page, making it easy to fill your page with content, expand your reach, and humanise your brand. Using your main Company hashtags and encouraging your staff to do the same whenever they post is also key.

It is important that your staff are trained effectively on how to act on a platform like LinkedIn®. Social selling is so powerful and yet I see so many companies place restrictions on their employees through social media policies that scare their staff into submission. They are so frightened of losing their job because they post something not in line with the company policy that they choose not to post at all. What a missed opportunity!

It is staggering to me that large enterprise companies are investing hundreds of thousands of ££ into LinkedIn® ads, and Sales Navigator licenses but not giving their marketing and sales teams the education and empowerment to turn this into real sales and ROI. I see it every week, large companies provide their people with a Formula One powerhouse sales tool like LinkedIn® Sales Navigator and they invest thousands into their staff, yet fail to train their people on how to win the social selling race.

Rant over. The point here is that you need to leverage your employees to spread your message far and wide on LinkedIn®, especially if you have more than 200 employees.

Inviting Your Connections to Follow your Page

At the time of writing this book, LinkedIn® is beta testing the ability to invite your connections to follow your LinkedIn® page. This will be a significant enhancement and will help to grow followers more quickly. At the moment it is a reactive process and therefore a slow process to grow your following if you aren't a household name brand. Unless you are willing to pay LinkedIn® for advertising to grow your followers.

LinkedIn® Pages to Follow

There are some fantastic brands out there and in my opinion these are some of the best LinkedIn® Pages to follow. You will get some great ideas, by following other LinkedIn® pages. There are at the time of writing this book more than 31.5million LinkedIn® Company pages on the LinkedIn® platform.

Start here on this link to explore LinkedIn® Pages in different sectors:

https://www.LinkedIn.com/company

The suggested pages below have some of the highest engagement and/or the biggest number of followers:

Zappos Family of Companies:

https://www.linkedin.com/company/zappos.com/

Amazon:

https://www.linkedin.com/company/amazon/

Nike:

https://www.linkedin.com/company/nike/

How to Create your LinkedIn® Company Page

To create a Company Page, click on *Work* in the top navigation bar of the LinkedIn® desktop version. At the very bottom of the menu, click *'Create a Company Page +'*.

Once you have done that, LinkedIn® will ask you to choose the type of page you want to create:

- Small business (fewer than 200 employees)

- Medium to large business (more than 200 employees)

- Showcase page (sub-pages associated with existing LinkedIn® pages)

- Educational institution (Schools / Universities)

As soon as you have selected your page type, you can begin to create your LinkedIn® Company Page. Start by entering the name of your company. LinkedIn® will let you know if that name is already taken. If it is, you will need to modify it to something unique. Keep in mind that you are limited to 100 characters.

Adding your company name will auto-fill your LinkedIn® Public URL using your company name. You can edit this, but it must still be unique. For ease and consistent branding, it is usually in your best interest to keep this as your company name.

The last field in the top section allows you to add the link to your company website. In the second section, you must fill in your *Company details*. Choose the appropriate choice for your industry, company size and company type.

The last section of your page details allows you to upload your company logo and add a tagline.

It looks best if the logo image is 300 X 300 pixels. It must be a JPEG or PNG format. Your tagline is like a headline for a Company page. You have 120 characters to write it. I recommend including some of your keywords in there to help your business to be found in search results.

Lastly, check the box to verify you are an official representative of the company. You will see a preview of your page on the right-hand side, then once you are happy with it, click the '*Create page*' button.

Now that your Company Page is Created, it's time to look at each section to make it fully complete or 'All Star' just like your personal profile.

1. Add a cover image. Click on the *pencil* icon to put your page into edit mode. Now you can upload, reposition or delete the image. The ideal dimensions of your LinkedIn® Page cover image are 1536 X 768 pixels.

2. You can add or edit the rest of your Company Page information by clicking the pencil icon to the right of your company name. Select *'Page info'* in the navigation area on the left, and make your changes to the name, logo and tagline of your LinkedIn® Page.

3. Go to the Overview section on the left to fill in or update your details. Be sure to include a complete company description which is required. Your description must be between 250 and 2,000 characters long, including spaces. As with your LinkedIn® personal profile, I would recommend you to use as many characters as possible.

4. Include information about your company, your products and services, who you help, problems that you solve for your clients and always keep your target market, ideal clients top of mind. Describe your company, bring in anything unique and credibility building. Anything compelling that will set you apart from your competitors. You may want to mention the key products and services that you provide. I would also recommend including some kind of 'call to action' telling people what you want them to do next.

5. Below this, you can add or edit the information about your company including your website, phone number, industry, company size, company type and year founded.

6. Now add specialities, you can add up to 20 specialties for your company. These are similar to skills in your personal profile. Think of keywords you want to be found for, reflecting what your company offers.

7. Finally, LinkedIn® will ask for 3 hashtags that your Company should be tagged for, choose the 3 most important hashtags and use the tips I gave earlier in Chapter 7 about hashtags to help you select the right ones.

Attract the Best Talent to your Company

Company Pages can be a great tool for recruiting and attracting great talent to your business. Having spent 13 years in the recruitment industry, LinkedIn® is a phenomenal tool for hiring. You can use all of the Boolean search tips I gave you to find great candidates as well as using LinkedIn®'s hiring features to advertise jobs on their platform.

Regardless of whether you have open roles or not, you should ALWAYS be recruiting. I am at any one time, hiring for 4 different roles. If I only recruited reactively it would be really hard work.

Because we recruit proactively, all the time, we always have a pool of great candidates to choose from when the time is right for them and us.

Your HR and recruitment teams need to be clued up on LinkedIn®. Your Hiring Managers need to know what they are doing on LinkedIn®. Building the bench of A & B players waiting in the wings to get started will save you time, energy and effort, and zero downtime when a role opens up.

I am always on the lookout for great people. I am looking for A player, enterprise sales candidates who may be looking for a move in the next 6 months. Please send your CV and a covering letter as to why I should consider you to careers@LinkedInbound.co.uk

In addition we are building and scaling our team of Marketing and Administrative talent, based out of our offices in the Midlands, once again to be considered, send your CV to careers@LinkedInbound.co.uk.

Recruitment and hiring can be a costly business, as well as time consuming. LinkedIn® can reduce your costs, speed up the recruitment cycle and help you attract amazing talent, it starts with having an attractive LinkedIn® page that will impress A players.

171

5 Actionable Insights:

1. Set up your Company Page and make sure it is fully completed 'All Star'
2. Create content every week for your LinkedIn® Page
3. Ensure all your staff have LinkedIn® their profile to your LinkedIn® Page
4. Ensure all your staff are following your LinkedIn® Page and sharing what you post
5. Always be recruiting, build your bench of A players and use LinkedIn® to seek the best

CHAPTER 10
Building Community in Groups

LinkedIn® groups have had a bad reputation over the last number of years. They became a place for spam and self-promotion and many LinkedIn® members left groups and migrated to forming communities on other platforms. With more than 1.9 million groups on LinkedIn®, feedback from users was that something had to change.

So, over the last 6 months, LinkedIn® has been making some adjustments to the way that groups operate, in an effort towards improving the quality and professional nature of their professional communities. Members after all crave real connection with peers, industry leaders and other LinkedIn® users who share the same interests as them.

In my opinion, the main value of being a member of other people's LinkedIn® groups comes in being able to connect and network with your target market. There can also be huge value in building your own community on the LinkedIn® platform should you choose to. I will cover both options in this chapter.

Types of Groups

Here are a few types of groups that you can currently find on LinkedIn®:

- Corporate Groups
- College / Event Alumni
- Non-Profit Groups
- Trade Organisations
- Conferences & Events
- Industry Specific Groups
- Networking Groups
- Geography Specific Groups
- Professional Bodies
- Job Title Specific Groups
- Shared Interest Groups

There are 'open' LinkedIn® groups where your application to join is automatic, with no vetting by a Group Manager. Then there are 'closed' LinkedIn® groups, where you have to request to join the group and have to be approved by a Group Manager. Closed groups tend to be more focused and niche, but there are some good open groups out there too.

I recommend that you are member of different types of groups. Always bear in mind that a Group Manager may vet you before letting you in to their community, so it's super important that you take the time to create a very credible and relevant LinkedIn® profile.

Which Groups am I Already in?

You can check out which groups you are already a member of here: http://LinkedIn.com/groups. You may not even have realised that you are in some of them!

Check that they are still relevant to what you currently do, and remove yourself from the ones which aren't. A way to assess the group is to look at how active the group is, go in and read recent discussions and see when the last discussion was posted. You can see a list group members in the top right of each group, so look at both the quantity of members as well as the quality. Some groups have over 500,000+ members, I would recommend sticking with more focused and niche groups relevant to your target market.

How Many Groups Should I be in?

You can be a member of up to 50 groups on LinkedIn® at one time, however you can leave a group at any time, so there's no harm in experimenting and trying different groups out.

Sometimes people will invite you to join a group by messaging you and inviting you to be a part of their community. Other times you will stumble across a group on another members profile, and think why not? Before long, you'll belong to dozens of groups. Just bear in mind that it's impossible to participate in a meaningful way in more than a few groups.

175

If you aren't getting the results you want, don't add more groups to your collection. Find a few groups that better suit your needs and leave the groups that don't. It is important to find and establish your top 5-10 groups and focus on being the most active in those.

You can be passive in the other groups, or use them for research or prospecting, which I talk about later in this chapter.

How to Search for Groups

You can use the search bar to look for groups, or you can go to the left-hand side of your home page (on the Desktop version).

LinkedIn® will also suggest them to you, and you can find interesting groups on the bottom of other members LinkedIn® profiles, if they have chosen to show them publicly.

You can also go to this link: http://LinkedIn.com/groups

At the end of the list of your current groups, there is a small link to search for and discover more groups. You can then use keywords and geography to search over 1.9 million groups.

Types of Group Posts

There are several ways to post in a group. They are similar to normal content posts, covered in Chapter 7. You can post photographs, videos, documents and text, the difference is that the post will only be seen by group members. In some cases the Group Manager may decide to 'Recommend' a specific post in the group. If that happens then all group members will see this in their notifications.

The more you help others in the group, the more you add value and deliver great content in a group, the more likely it is that you will get on the radar of the Group Manager. It is always a good idea to connect with them and start to build that relationship. Become more visible in your core focus groups, and more credible by posting interesting, thought-provoking ideas and great discussion points. You could not possibly do this in every single group you are a member of, so be strategic, pick the groups where your target market is most prevalent and use this opportunity to attract more views to your profile and potentially leads.

Whether you join an industry or profession specific group, a target market group or set up your own, the number one rule is that you contribute positively. Never ever hard sell or spam the members. This will damage your reputation, so stay professional and focus on giving and helping others. Share useful and relevant content and engage other group members with your knowledge, information and expertise.

Anyone who is perceived to be spamming a group will be relegated to a penalty box, or can be booted out of the group altogether. This privilege of acting against spammers not only extends to the group manager but to all the other group members as well. Any group member has the power to report or remove conversations that they believe don't meet the guidelines of LinkedIn®, and can block other members.

Every conversation that you have on LinkedIn® will now be published automatically without any approval from the manager of the group. However the manager of a LinkedIn® group can still remove the post, marking specific people as required in moderation.

Respond to Discussions in Groups

You can use the LinkedIn® groups to your advantage by looking out for conversations started by other members in the group, where people are looking for help on a subject which you know a great deal about.

Always remember to respond to discussions with useful advice, in a 'non-salesy' way to help the other person solve their issue. Always remember that social selling is the art of selling without selling. A group is a great place to start a new business relationship and if your focus groups are filled with people in your target market, you never know what can happen.

Be a part of the conversation, look at the answers of other people, create debate, join in and add value, add value and then more value. As with all content on LinkedIn® you can tag others in comments, to bring more people that you know in the group into the conversation.

Using Groups for Prospecting

One of my favourite things about groups, is the ability to message other members in the group, even if you are not connected to them as a 1st degree connection. This is so powerful for prospecting, as you can reach out to people who are potentially indoor?? 3rd degree network and beyond who previously were unreachable.

Look at the groups where your target market hangs out. Then work your way through the list of members and look at their profiles. Use the prospecting techniques I have already given you in previous chapters to add these people to your LinkedIn® network. It's another great source of potential clients.

Should you Create your Own Group?

Creating a group is not for everyone.

If you already own and manage a community on Facebook, then you should consider a LinkedIn® Group.

This is a potentially huge reputation building opportunity, there are a number of reasons you may want to consider creating a group:

- Serve and help your target market

- Serve and help your existing clients

- Control who gets in, so you can lock out your competitors

- Build a community around your brand

- Increase your visibility and credibility

If you do decide to create a group, find a niche that no-one else is fulfilling and dedicate time to set it up and manage it well. You will need to dedicate time to approving new members, if you decide to make it a closed group. Check in once a week on pending requests and approve those that you want to let in. If you do decide to set up your own group, remember to keep your group page fresh with new content. There is no excuse for an inactive page.

Create discussion points and posts regularly to stimulate the conversation. In most communities your members will contribute too. If you have someone in your team who can act as a Community Manager then make them a Group Admin and give them the responsibility of keeping the group active.

When you create your group, give it a catchy and relevant name. Set up the 'About' section of the group, so that members of LinkedIn® can decide if they want to join. Add a group header image and create a logo for the group. Having a group logo makes the community look more professional and it will appear on the profile of LinkedIn® members who belong to your group if they choose to show this. You can create specific group rules which each member needs to abide by, in order to be a member of your community. Once your group has been set up on LinkedIn®, it will have its own URL, so you can use that link to invite people in your network to join your LinkedIn® community.

I currently have 2 separate groups on LinkedIn®, one dedicated to my Social Selling Academy and one for those who have attended my LinkedIn® Masterclass. By building these communities, I can keep my most important raving fans in the loop, I can stay top of mind with them and continue to serve and help my clients.

Final Word on Groups

Be active and proactive. Keep content current. Engage. Don't underestimate the power of groups. LinkedIn® are still making changes to improve them and I am predicting a resurgence. So be an early adopter, figure out your strategy for LinkedIn® groups and decide if you want to be active or passive, be a member or a group manager with your own community.

5 Actionable Insights:

1. Check which groups you are already a member of.
2. Search for new groups and add yourself as member of groups relevant to you.

3. Practice adding group members in your target market to your LinkedIn® network.
4. Choose your top 5-10 Groups in which to focus on being an active member.
5. Decide if you want to create your own LinkedIn® Group

CHAPTER 11
Premium vs. Sales Navigator

Everything in this book so far has been written for the FREE version of LinkedIn®, as many people who pick up this book are new to LinkedIn® and just starting out on their social selling journey.

There are, however, several paid options to choose from on LinkedIn®. It helps to understand the breadth of the LinkedIn® offering, each is targeted at users in different situations:

Recruiters: The LinkedIn® Recruiter Lite and Recruiter Corporate are essential tools for recruiters. I've not met a true recruiter who does not subscribe to the LinkedIn® Recruiter offering. Having spent 13 years in the recruitment industry, these are premium products. Most of the agencies I work with as well as corporate clients have these solutions.

Job Seekers: If recruiters find the tools valuable, similarly so do job seekers. The Job Seeker licence allows you to be seen as a featured applicant, compare yourself to other candidates, and send messages directly to recruiters. You'll also see everyone who has viewed your profile.

Professionals: The three levels for general use are (1) Free, (2) Premium, and (3) Sales Navigator. The major difference here is how deeply and with how much detail you can see your extended network, your ability to outreach to a wider network as well as the search functions which give greater granularity than the free version. We have already covered the free version at length, so what do you get if you decide to upgrade?

LinkedIn®'s Premium Offering

Premium for business, includes 15 InMail messages, advanced search filters, unlimited searches in your extended network and additional company data. Personally, I would suggest that if you are going to pay for LinkedIn®, that premium is not the option to go for. I would always recommend Sales Navigator, because for an extra $20 / £20 a month you move from a BMW to a Formula One driving machine that will catapult your sales results to the next level, IF you apply what I teach in this book about prospecting and content.

LinkedIn®'s Sales Navigator Offering

"Sales Navigator allows sales professionals to tap into the power of LinkedIn® efficiently. It improves social selling in support of powerful daily habits," Diana Kucer, LinkedIn®'s Director of Global Product Marketing.

Besides making it really easy for your sales team to get connected with prospects and pan out a list of ideal connections, it can do a lot more for your business. If you have had the time to check LinkedIn® sales navigator, you would have read their tag line, which correctly explains the motive of social selling and the navigator itself. The tag line says, 'You know the art of selling. We can help with the science'. It is not just hit and trial method or cold calling tactics that run this particular amazing tool. It has sophisticated background algorithms; to give you lead recommendations which are customised as per your business needs and prospect profiles. Sales Navigator is a social selling offering from LinkedIn® that can have an immediate, and dramatic impact on results for most businesses. It allows you to find hidden decision makers at large accounts and engage with them based on their LinkedIn® activity.

Here is a list of all the features included with Sales Navigator:

- Easily find new and promising leads with advanced search options

- **Get real-time sales updates about your prospects and customers**

- Unlock full profiles for leads who aren't in your network

- See who has shown interest in your products and services, view their profiles

185

- Reach out to other members with InMail option

- Measure and track your social selling efforts with Social Selling Index (SSI) dashboard

- Build trusted relationships with colleagues and other members

- Earn quick and easy recommendations from other team members

- Reach out to different verticals and professionals across globe

- Cross selling benefits to accompany your products and services

- Focus on the right people, reach them at the most appropriate time of selling

- **Unlimited search results with additional filters such as postcode and headcount**

- **The ability to save leads (people) and track their activity**

- **The ability to save accounts (companies) and track their activity**

- **'View Similar 'will give you an additional 100 suggested profiles**

- Get amazing insights on the go with mobile app availability

- **Create and save lists based on your Boolean searches**

The features in bold are my absolute favourites. If you have ever hit the commercial search limit on LinkedIn® you will love that you can run unlimited searches. If you work very regionally specific, then you will love being able to search within a 10-15 mile radius of a specific postcode.

If you only want to prospect large companies, then you will love the fact that you can filter by size of company based on their headcount. And if you are prospecting heavily then you will adore the saved lists, meaning you can just jump back in and start prospecting again without having to re-type in your Boolean searches.

LinkedIn®'s Sales Navigator Team Edition

For those reading this from larger companies, Sales Navigator also comes in a multi-seat version, Sales Navigator Team, which includes 30 InMail messages, 25 Out-of-Network profile unlocks, 10 PointDrive presentations and more. Sales Navigator

Enterprise offers unlimited seats, 50 InMail messages per month, per seat, 25 Out-of-Network profile unlocks, unlimited PointDrive presentations and advanced admin functionality. Sales Navigator Enterprise also includes Salesforce integration.

Many of my Corporate Clients have the Team edition and for a sales organisation it can be a great way to motivate and drive competition, leveraging the SSI leaderboard as long as the team are fully trained in how to use it effectively. Enterprise sales of LinkedIn® Sales Navigator are handled by Account Managers at LinkedIn®'s headquarters, and prices will depend on the total number of licences and how good your negotiating skills are.

InMail's can be advantageous for those hard to reach and out of network contacts, however an InMail if used in the wrong way to pitch and sell will always be ignored or deleted. InMail to me screams 'I am trying to sell you something' so I avoid using them by personal choice, I always connect at 2nd degree in the way I showed you in the prospecting chapters.

Sales Navigator 30-Day Free Trial

LinkedIn® has done something very smart with Sales Navigator. You can get a free trial for one-month to test it out for yourself. This demonstrates how confident the company is that Sales Navigator can have a tangible impact on your business.

A word of warning, when you first sign up, LinkedIn® will ask for your credit card details and will automatically select the annual plan, which means if you forget to cancel or don't want to continue with the trial your card will be swiped for the full annual amount. So be sure to change it to the monthly plan if you want to pay monthly. You can cancel at any time and are not tied in for any length of time. If you have previously taken a trial, you will have to wait a full 12 months to be able to take a trial again.

I do recommend taking a trial of the Sales Navigator tool, but only once you truly understand the free version. You can get results as a free user, but you will speed up the process and be more efficient with your time as a Sales Navigator licence holder.

I cover Sales Navigator training at length in my 3 Day Social Selling Masterclass, and when I deliver in-house training for large companies, they usually already have LinkedIn® Sales Navigator licences so I dedicate some of the time to walking through the features and additional benefits over the free version.

More Information:

You can access the sale pages about LinkedIn® Sales Navigator here:

https://business.LinkedIn.com/sales-solutions/sales-navigator

You can stay up to date with all of the latest product features here:

189

https://business.LinkedIn.com/sales-solutions/product-update

For eBooks and sales tips provided by LinkedIn® click here:

https://business.LinkedIn.com/sales-solutions/sales-strategies-tips#ebooks

To watch webinars on social selling from within LinkedIn®'s resources click here:

https://business.LinkedIn.com/sales-solutions/sales-strategies-tips#webinars

5 Actionable Insights:

1. Take the 30-day free trial of Sales Navigator once you feel comfortable with LinkedIn®

2. Practice running advanced searches for Leads (People) with the extra filters

3. Practice running advanced searches for Accounts (Companies) with the extra filters

4. Save your Leads and Accounts to specific lists and start receiving updates on them

5. Decide if you want to become a long-term Sales Navigator licence holder

CHAPTER 12
Planning: Social Selling Habits

The key to success with any form of social selling on any platform is consistency. Your LinkedIn® SSI can go up just as quickly as it can go down. LinkedIn® membership is like a gym membership, you've actually got to go to the gym, listen to the instructors, follow a system, use the equipment and be consistent to get any kind of results.

It's the same with LinkedIn®, you need to be active on LinkedIn® daily, not just when you feel like it. You need to show up, be there, engage with people in your network, build relationships, deliver great content and be consistent with your outreach to prospects for it to actually work.

Don't expect instant results, it could happen but it's more likely that it will be 3-6 months of implementation before you start to see things change. Why? Because it takes time to build up your personal brand, it takes time to grow your visibility and increase your credibility. It takes patience and consistency to build up a network of prospects in your exact target market, and then with some testing and trialling different approaches it's going to take some time before you start to get regular responses to your outreach.

However, if you do apply the daily, weekly and monthly habits I am going to give you in this chapter, CONSISTENTLY, you will start to see results.

So let's look at planning for success, and that starts with habits. There are a couple of great books on this topic, my favourite being 'The Power of Habit' by Charles Duhigg. So I won't even attempt to educate you on this topic, he does a much better job than me.

I have designed these habits for you to be able to achieve them in as little time as possible, from just 20 minutes a day. If you choose to spend more time then you will supercharge your results.

I am a believer that what gets scheduled, gets done! It is very important to block out time in your calendar each day, week and month to ensure that these tasks happen.

5 Daily Habits

Each day here are the key things to focus on, all of which will help you drive up your LinkedIn® Social Selling Index (SSI), in just 20 minutes a day:

1. Log in to LinkedIn® either on your desktop or on the mobile app

2. Check your inbox for new messages and respond (2-5 minutes)

3. Create one post, in line with the content strategies shared in Chapter 7 (5 minutes)

4. Like, Comment and Share on others posts from within your network. Engage with their content and engage with or create discussions on others posts (1-3 minutes)

5. Run a boolean search and find 10 prospects in your target market, send them a personalised connection request. (10 minutes)

5 Weekly Habits

Each week here are the key things to focus on, all of which will help you to drive up your LinkedIn® Social Selling Index, in just 30 mins a week:

1. Give a recommendation to someone else in your 1st degree network (3 mins)

2. Check your Social Selling Index (SSI) overall score and track it (2 mins)

3. Go through your inbox and respond to all people who have accepted your connection request, then send your chosen follow up 2nd message (15 mins)

4. Track your conversion rate of invitation to acceptance (ideally this should be somewhere between 50-70%) (5 minutes)

5. Track your conversion rate of 2nd message to positive response (ideally this should be between 3-8%) (5 minutes)

3 Monthly Habits

Each month here are the key things to focus on, all of which will help you to drive up your LinkedIn® Social Selling Index, in just 1-hour month:

1. Write an Article to help to position you as an expert in your field. (30-45 Mins)

2. Back up your data by downloading a copy of your connections. (2 Mins)

3. Check all your LinkedIn® statistics and track them including profile views, search appearances, average post views, SSI trends

As with anything new, where consistency is required, it's always good to have an accountability partner. Why not share this book with a close friend, business partner, client or contact and ask them to be your accountability partner.

Ideally pick someone who is highly competitive and challenge them to an SSI race! Run a 90 Day Challenge to see who can create the highest SSI, that way you can be sure that you will be implementing your habits and have some fun at the same time!

CHAPTER 13
Plus: Additional LinkedIn® Learning

I absolutely love learning new things, especially on topics that can help me to grow my business, so I have provided some additional resources for you to get additional learning tools and materials if you want to continue to broaden your knowledge of LinkedIn® and Social Selling.

Visit the LinkedIn® Help Centre

If you are ever stuck on any aspect of LinkedIn® and you don't have this book to hand, then you can always visit the LinkedIn® Help Centre. You can find this link in the top right-hand corner of your LinkedIn® profile, under the menu called 'Me'. Or you can access the LinkedIn® Help Centre here: http://help.LinkedIn.com

Follow the Official LinkedIn® Blog

You can read the official LinkedIn® Blog on this link. It will always keep you up to date with the latest updates and changes happening on LinkedIn®: http://blog.linkedin.com

LinkedIn® Learning Centre

This is a section of LinkedIn® that few people know about. LinkedIn® has an entire resource centre where you can learn about so many topics! There are literally hundreds of online courses in business, creativity, entrepreneurship, technology, marketing and so much more. You need to be a paid user of LinkedIn® to access this.

You will find this learning centre in the top right corner on the desktop version of LinkedIn®, under the icon with nine small squares (the same place you found groups earlier). Or you can click on this link to be taken there:

https://www.linkedin.com/learning

Subscribe to my YouTube Channel

I am working with the UK's leading YouTube strategist, David Walsh.

We are on journey together to create the best and most subscribed to YouTube channel on the subject of LinkedIn® and Social Selling. I would absolutely love you to continue your learning there.

Just hit 'SUBSCRIBE' here: http://youtube.com and set the notifications to 'on' so that you are notified every time I add a new video to help you.

Many thanks in advance for doing this. My goal is to reach 10,000 subscribers this year so that I can have the biggest impact and help as many people as possible.

If you have ideas for videos or topics then get in touch with me on LinkedIn® or send an email to hello@LinkedInbound.co.uk.

Attend my 1-Day 'Get Your LinkedIn® Profile Sorted!' Workshop

As mentioned in Chapter 2, I run monthly 1-Day workshops called *'Get Your LinkedIn® Profile Sorted!'*.

Due to my international reach and my mission to create £1billion in sales for my clients, these workshops are live streamed each month. People also attend in person in the room with me at my headquarters in Derby, East Midlands, UK.

Typically SMEs with an SSI of less than 50, come to my 1-day workshop frustrated that they just aren't getting enough leads, with no idea where their next sale is coming from.
Many are overwhelmed, trying to juggle everything in their business and they just can't seem to find the time to do everything. Others are trying to build their personal brand and position themselves as the 'go-to' expert in their field, but just don't know where to start.

If you are still not sure on your exact target market or where to start when it comes to your LinkedIn® profile, then you would probably benefit from spending a full day with me.

You can book online at https://www.linkedinbound.co.uk to *'Get Your LinkedIn® Profile sorted!'*.

Attend my 'Ultimate 3-Day LinkedIn® Social Selling Masterclass'

A highly practical deep dive into 8 Social Selling Strategies, that deliver you Inbound Leads, Brand Awareness & Sales Opportunities from the LinkedIn® Platform.

The Ultimate 3-Day LinkedIn® 'Social Selling' Masterclass, gives you an amazing 3 days with me. This is the ONLY 3-day LinkedIn® training of its kind in the UK. In the last 12 months, this content has generated in excess of £8.3 million for delegates who have attended and applied my knowledge.

I look forward to welcoming you into the Linked Inbound headquarters, in the East Midlands for an unforgettable experience. Not only will you learn how to unlock LinkedIn®, you will also network and build relationships with other delegates on the course.

Included in your ticket, on Day 1 you will be treated to a champagne reception overlooking the beautiful weir at the award-winning Darley's restaurant. On Day 2 you will experience a divine 3 course meal in the same venue. I cannot wait to host you.

You can book online at https://www.linkedinbound.co.uk/book/ to 'Get Your LinkedIn® Profile sorted!'

Ask me for Help

If this book has overwhelmed you, but you know that LinkedIn® should be high on your agenda for B2B lead generation, then explore if we have a solution for you. We only take on 5 new clients a month and there is a waiting list to get started. In addition, there is a strict criteria that a business needs to meet before we can do business together. My advice would be to check through this list first before applying to have a conversation with me about how I can help.

1. You have an established business, trading for at least 3 years

2. Your LinkedIn® network is at least 1000 connections for the profile you want to use for LinkedIn® prospecting

3. You are already a Sales Navigator license holder or are willing to purchase Sales Navigator from LinkedIn®

4. You have a product or service that we can easily generate an ROI (return on investment). High value, high ticket products and services work best

5. You are really clear on your exact target market, and are open to coaching and advice on this from a LinkedIn® perspective

6. You are willing to attend a 3-Day Social Selling Masterclass with me in Derby, within the first 90 Days of your outsourced campaign starting. This usually costs £1997 + VAT, however one ticket is included complimentary, if you are selected as a client

7. You see social selling and prospecting through LinkedIn® as a strategic activity that builds your sales pipeline for the long term and not a 'quick fix' or 'magic bullet'

8. You have the funds to pay for a full year and are committed to a partnership with us for a minimum of 12 months. The investment starts at *£1000 + VAT per month, with a *£1000 + VAT set up fee (*Prices subject to change. These are correct at the time of publishing this book.)

9. You have the capacity to follow up the leads we help you generate, and have a sales process in place to move the leads from the online conversation we create into an offline phone call or meeting

10. And finally, we need to be able to get on with each other. We only do business with companies and people who

hold the same values as we do. We can only determine this once we start to build our relationship and that starts with an initial discovery call.

To book a discovery call to speak with me personally, click here to book in a time that suits you best.

http://calendly.com/meetsamrathling/discovery

Note: *My diary gets booked up way in advance so time slots are limited. We also request a £100 deposit for each discovery call. If you meet the criteria and move forwards as a Pipeline Pro client, we put this towards your set up fee. If we are not a good fit for each other and you do not proceed for whatever reason, we refund your deposit. This has been put in place to protect my time and ensure that you are committed to this and serious about taking your LinkedIn® lead generation to the next level.*

Book Sam to Train your Team or Speak at your Conference

Simply send an email to hello@LinkedInbound.co.uk with the dates, numbers of people you need trained and my team will come back to you to book in a time for us to speak and learn more about what you are looking for.

Share your Results

I would like to thank you for reading this book, which I hope you have found useful. Over time, as you implement the steps, you will start to see your LinkedIn® SSI improving, more people visiting your profile, your appearance in search results increasing and your ability to engage, connect and build relationships through LinkedIn® getting easier.

The impact and effectiveness of your social selling will over time start to win you more clients, new opportunities and help you to grow your business. If you do secure new business from LinkedIn®, share it with me in a LinkedIn® message.

Remember that massive mission I am on? I want you to be a part of my £1billion goal, so connect with me and reach out with your wins and successes.

My hope is that you now feel that you are totally LinkedIn® and not LinkedOut!

About the Author

Sam Rathling

Sam Rathling was born in Kent in the South of England and now lives in the East Midlands. Her Dad was a Bank Manager for 25 years so she spent most of her childhood moving home and changing schools. Each time her Dad was promoted, she had to make friends all over again, in a new place. Sam has essentially been networking since she was 5 years old. Sam describes networking in its simplest form as turning strangers into friends. Building relationships is a core part of Sam's strengths and she is a masterful networker.

Sam is a Mum to three children, Oscar, Maya and Liliana. They are the reason she became an Entrepreneur and form a huge part of her WHY? Everything she is working for and building is a legacy for her kids. When she is not working or travelling the world delivering social selling strategies and LinkedIn® training to sold out events or in-house with Corporate Clients she spends quality time with her kids. Sam has two younger sisters, who now live in Australia and New Zealand.

An Amazon best-selling Author and International Speaker, she gets booked to speak at conferences months in advance, her 1-Day Workshops called 'Get Your LinkedIn® Profile Sorted!' and her 'Ultimate 3-Day Social Selling LinkedIn® Masterclass' sell out every month with delegates from across the world. Sam consults with multi-billion Corporate Clients globally, delivering consultancy on social selling, in-house Masterclasses and outsourced solutions.

Sam is the CVO (Chief Visionary Officer) of Linked Inbound Limited, the fastest growing LinkedIn® Marketing Agency in Europe. She leads a team of LinkedIn® 'ninjas' who are experts at helping her clients get results from LinkedIn®. Her amazing team are based from the Linked Inbound headquarters in Derby, led by Operations Director, Andoly Rathling. Backed by a multi-national group of companies and surrounded by incredible mentors and business advisors, Sam is on a mission to generate over £1billion for her clients from LinkedIn®.

To learn more about Sam Rathling or to book her for your event visit SamRathling.com.

To book a 1-Day Workshop visit http://linkedinbound.co.uk/book/

To book a 3-Day Ultimate Social Selling Masterclass visit http://linkedinbound.co.uk/bookultimate/

To discuss your LinkedIn® outreach with Sam and her team, book an appointment at:
http://calendly.com/meetsamrathling/discovery/

To book Sam to train your team in-house, send an email to:
hello@linkedinbound.co.uk or call +44 (0)1332 653 659.

205

Connect with Sam on Social Media

Sam is keen to connect with all of her readers, so please feel free to reach out and connect on any or all of the following:

Subscribe to Sam's YouTube Channel:

http://youtube.com/samrathling

Connect with Sam on LinkedIn®:

https://uk.LinkedIn.com/in/samrathling-LinkedIn®expert

Follow Sam on Twitter: http://twitter.com/samrathling

Like Sam's Facebook Page: http://facebook.com/samrathling

Follow Sam on Instagram: http://instagram.com/samrathling

Amazon Author Central Page:

http://www.amazon.com/Sam-Rathling/e/B00BU93ZD4

More from Sam Rathling

To get your paperback copy of the book "GIVE: 16 Giving Strategies To Grow Your Business click here:

Amazon.co.uk Customers:
http://amzn.to/10GcF95
Amazon.com Customers:
http://amzn.to/10Xcaq5

If you prefer the digital version then use these links to get the full digital version:

Amazon.co.uk Customers: http://amzn.to/YkaE7d
Amazon.com Customers: http://amzn.to/167XVnC

If you don't have a Kindle you can use this link to download the free Kindle reading App: http://amzn.to/XTHawP

Before you Go...

It's now the end of this book, and hopefully now you feel more confident and informed about how to generate leads from LinkedIn®. My hope is that you learned something new and found this book useful and inspiring.

If you believe that others would benefit from my methodology, I would really appreciate a review of this book on Amazon.

Thank you in advance for doing this for us, it means more to me than you realise.

Made in the USA
Coppell, TX
23 January 2020

14907817R00122